BADMINTON

Sixth Edition

Tony Grice

american press
Boston, Massachusetts
www.americanpresspublishers.com

Acknowledgements

I wish to thank USA Badminton and the BWF for their permission to reprint the official USAB and IBF rules, also known as the Laws of Badminton.

Special gratitude goes to Larry Lambert for providing the section on skill testing. Special appreciation is also expressed to Ferris Bavousett, Don Stevenson and Warren K. Emerson, former Editor of Badminton USA, for their fine photography. Special thanks goes to Mr. Stevenson for the cover photograph.

I also wish to thank Cheryl Northam, Chris Sampson, Bill Connatser, Doug Pepping, Ben Telesca, Jennifer Melgar, Gina Markin, and Shannon Bruce for their aid in demonstrating various skills throughout the text.

I also wish to thank my family for their support and encouragement, as well as, the helpful criticisms and suggestions from my colleagues at numerous universities.

Preface

The purpose of this book is to assist the college student in learning how to perform and enjoy the game of badminton at all levels of play. It includes an organized description of the fundamental skills and advanced techniques in badminton. Each chapter is designed to both graphically and visually demonstrate all of the aspects needed by the college student to play badminton.

Drawings, diagrams and photographs clearly illustrate the foot, hand and body positions essential to badminton. New updated chapters on history, the scoring and rules of badminton, and conditioning and weight training are also included. Review questions at the end of the text provide examples which clarify the content of the textbook.

The sixth edition of *Badminton* has been revised with new figures and photographs and includes the latest USAB rules. New appendices provide a glossary of terms, selected references including books, magazines and films, the complete USBA list of 2007. Publications and a complete list of USAB and BWF Associations. This information should be of special interest to the badminton teacher and coach.

The author hopes that this textbook covers all of the basics that students need to play badminton.

About the Author . . .

Tony Grice received his B.S.E. and M.Ed. from Memphis State University and the Ed.D. from Northwestern State University of Louisiana. Grice has been a high school teacher and coach and a college varsity badminton coach. He has taught badminton at all levels several universities.

He has also conducted numerous badminton instructional clinics in the United States, Guatemala and Mexico. Grice has served as a member of the Board of Directors for the USA Badminton (USAB) and as the National Team Exercise Physiologist for the USAB. He traveled with the U.S. National Team to the 1987 World Championships in Beijing, China as the team trainer and also served as the manager for the South Team at the 1989 Olympic Festival in Oklahoma City. Grice also served as an Official Umpire for the United States Olympic Sports Festivals for 1993 and 1995 held in San Antonio, Texas, and in Boulder, Colorado respectively.

Grice has been a nationally ranked player and has competed as a player internationally. He was ranked nationally as high as 15th in Open Men's Singles and 11th in Open Men's Doubles. Grifce recently won the 40+ Mixed Doubles and the 60+ Men's Doubles at the 2008 Senior National Badminton Championships and previously won the 50+ Men's Singles in 1998 and the 50+ Men's Doubles in both 1998 and 1999.

Contents

xi

APPENDICES

Nature and History of the Game

1

NATURE OF THE GAME

Badminton appeals to people of all ages and levels of skill, to both sexes, and for leisure activity as well as competition. The sport may be played indoors and out-of-doors. The badminton participant must possess various degrees of agility, cardiorespiratory endurance, flexibility, muscular strength and muscular endurance. The casual, average or expert player will hopefully understand and appreciate the benefits that are derived from badminton socially, as well as, physically and mentally.

Badminton is a sport involving striking techniques and strokes that vary greatly from relatively slow to quick and deceptive movements. Since the shuttlecock does not bounce and must be played in the air, it makes for a fast game requiring quick reflexes and some conditioning. Indeed, when played by experts, it is considered to be the fastest court game in the world, with smashes of over 200 miles per hour having been recorded. However, both singles and doubles play may be controlled to meet individual needs and abilities. From your neighborhood backyard badminton match to a Thomas Cup Match played in a country where badminton is the national sport with thousands of screaming fans, it is an enjoyable sport to be played for physical activity throughout one's life.

HISTORY OF THE GAME

The exact origin of badminton is unknown. A game played in China using a shuttlecock object dates back more than 2000 years. This ancient Chinese game of shuttlecock kicking called **Ti Jian Zi** was played in China around the First Century B.C. It usually involved hitting the shuttle with either hands or feet and eventually evolved into using various other implements as well. Records of different countries show that a game with wooden paddles and a shuttlecock was played in ancient China, on the royal court of England in the twelfth century, in the early eighteenth century in Poland, and in India later in the nineteenth century.

A badminton-like game called **battledore and shuttlecock** was played in Europe between the eleventh and fourteenth centuries. Medieval woodcut drawings depict a shuttlecock being batted with wooden paddles. The bat or battledore was a derivative of the Old English word for cudgel which is translated as an instrument for beating or striking. Battledore and shuttlecock required the participants to keep the shuttle in play as long as possible. Shakespeare mentions this game by name in several of his writings. In seventeenth century France, the game of shuttlecock was called **jeu de volant.** Similar battledore-type games were observed in Poland, Germany and other European countries during the late seventeenth and early eighteenth centuries. **Poona** was another game using a shuttle which was developed by British officers stationed in Poona, India around 1870. Coincidentally, this was approximately the time that the name **Badminton** became associated with and substituted for battledore-shuttlecock in England.

During the 1860's, battledore and shuttlecock was being played in Badminton House, a great hall of the Somerset family in Gloucestershire, England. The playing area of this front hall in Badminton House was more narrow at the middle than at the two ends. This "hourglass" shape apparently suggested the need for playing the shuttle at a minimum height in order to keep the rally going. A string was later added across the middle of the hall to make an elementary net. The game of badminton continued to be played on this "waisted" shaped court until 1901. The original rules of the game were standardized in 1887 and later revised in 1895 and again in 1905. These revised rules still govern the sport today, except for minor changes.

Ironically, the oldest continuous badminton club in existence is located in the United States. The Badminton Club of New York was organized during the winter of 1878-1879 and remains active today. The Badminton Association of England was the first national organization for promoting badminton. It was established in 1893 and held the first **All-England Championships** in 1897. Badminton spread rapidly throughout Great Britain and then to northern Europe, North America and the Far East. The presence of the British military influence in most parts of the world assisted greatly in promoting its popularity.

Today, the game of badminton is governed world-wide by the **World Badminton Federation** (WBF). The WBF was originally the **International Badminton Federation** (IBF) and was founded in 1934 with nine member nations. The IBF adopted its new name, World Badminton Federation, effective January, 2007. the WBF has grown to over 156 member nations and claims over fifty million members. There are eight international organizations within the I.B.F. including five geographical bodies for Africa, Asia, Europe, Pan America and Oceania. The W.B.F. is governed by the General Meeting of delegates from each member National Organization. The role of this body has changed dramatically since the early days of strictly amateur play. Six committees sub-divide responsibilities as follows: Business; Development; Finance; Open Badminton; and the Rules and Laws of Badminton. These committees influence almost every aspect of the game, including the coordination and supervision of: (1) national and international tournaments and international matches; (2) world tournaments (both for individual players and for national teams); (3) the manufacture of shuttles, rackets and court equipment; (4) advertising by players on court, as well as, court dress, sports medicine and drug testing; (5) training and certifying qualified tournament officials (referees, umpires and lines persons); (6) coaching and assistance for developing countries; (7) interpreting and up-dating the Laws of Badminton; and (8) the promotion of badminton with publicity and public relations. The major events organized by the W.B.F. are as follows: the Men's World Team Badminton Championships for the Thomas Cup; the Ladies' World Team Championships for the Uber Cup; the World Individual Championships; the Mixed Team Championship for the Sudirman Cup; and the Super Series.

The **Super Series** is a major step by the WBF to generate more interest in badminton around the world. The Super Series will consist of twelve Open events, with a minimum of $200,000 in prize money in each event. These will serve as the qualifiers for the season ending Super Series Finals which will be the richest ever badminton tournament, offering $500,000 in prize money.

Only the top eight singles and top eight pairs in doubles and mixed doubles would qualify for the Finals. Plus a maximum of two players per country can qualify for the Finals. The number of entries for each category in the twelve events is limited to 32, of which four qualify as at-large entries. In the Finals, the national separation rule normally used in all the Super Series events has been eliminated. Therefore, two players from the same country may meet as early as the first round.

Increased television coverage worldwide is guaranteed by requiring each host to provide for the live telecast of the semi-final and final rounds. In addition, Sports Media Promotions, the marketing agents for the Super Series, will produce 36 half-hour programs to be telecast in major markets around the world in a further attempt to elevate the profile of badminton.

The **Thomas Cup** is the most prestigious trophy in world badminton for men. The Thomas Cup was presented by Sir George Thomas in 1947. It has been contested 20 times since 1948-49. The **Uber Cup** represents the most prestigious trophy in world badminton for women. It was presented by Mrs. Betty Uber in 1956 and has been contested 12 times since 1956-57. It is now organized in conjunction with the Thomas Cup. Both competitions are held on a two year cycle in the even years. In 1977, the first **World Individual Championships** were held in Maalmo, Sweden. These were held for the second time at Jakarta, Indonesia in 1980 and again in 1983 at Copenhagen, Denmark. Since then, the World Individual Championships have been competed for in the odd-numbered years and thus alternate every other year with the Thomas Cup and the Uber Cup Championships. The 2005 World Individual Championships were held in Anahein, CA. Notably, the U.S. won the men's doubles title. The next World Badminton Championships will be in Glasgow, Scotland for 2007. The **Sudirman Cup** for the World Mixed Doubles Championship began in Jakarta, Indonesia in 1989 and is held in connection with the World Individual Championships during the odd years.

Badminton has been a relatively unappreciated sport in the United States. Although introduced in New York in 1878, the sport developed slowly. Interest increased during World War I when Canadian and American soldiers observed the sport in England. Badminton popularity in the U.S. reached an all-time high during the 1930's. Canada's interest in badminton along with several Hollywood movie stars' attraction to the game helped greatly in promoting the game. Jess Willard, a professional badminton player from Boston, toured all over the U.S.

and visited Hollywood in the early 1930's. Willard is said to have given instruction to several Hollywood stars and their families. The first national organization in the U.S. was the **American Badminton Association** (A.B.A.). It was formed in 1936 and sponsored the first U.S. National Championships in 1937 in Chicago. Enthusiasm seemed to decrease following World War II, due possibly to a lack of facilities. However, the first national junior tournament was held in 1947 and in 1949, David G. Freeman, retired undefeated in his ten-year badminton career by winning the U.S. Championship, the All-England Championship, and all of his Thomas Cup matches. Freeman is considered the best American player ever and arguably the greatest badminton player of all time. The U.S. men's team continued to play well throughout the fifties. making the final round of Thomas Cup several times. Joe Alston even made the cover of *Sports Illustrated* in 1956. The United States' women held the Uber Cup from 1957 through 1966. The first national collegiate championship was held in 1970. Throughout the seventies, the Association for Intercollegiate Athletics for Women (A.I.A.W.) played an integral role in promoting badminton at the college level. Numerous colleges and universities awarded full, four-year athletic scholarships to both men and women. When the A.I.A.W. was disbanded in 1979 and the National Collegiate Athletic Association (N.C.A.A.) took over governance of women's collegiate sports, badminton in the U.S. lost a very strong ally and supporter of college badminton.

Reprinted by permission of UFS, Inc.

In the 1970's, badminton continued to grow but at a slower rate. Interest and money in professional sports increased geometrically during this period, but the general public's perception of badminton as a slow-paced, leisurely game was and is truly a misconception. However, in recent years, interest has increased substantially. The A.B.A. was reorganized and in 1977 became the **United States Badminton Association** (U.S.B.A.). In 1985, the game of Badminton was adopted as a full medal sport for the Olympic Games of 1992 in Barcelona, Spain. This followed its presentation as a demonstration sport in the 1988 Olympics in Seoul, Korea. The inclusion of badminton as an Olympic sport encourages optimism for its future popularity, recognition and success. The U.S.B.A. was the National Governing Body (N.G.B.) representing badminton in the United States Olympic Committee (U.S.O.C.). However, in 1996, the U.S.B.A. adopted a new name, **USA Badminton**, primarily for marketing purposes.

Currently, the best players in the world come from China, Europe, Korea, Malaysia and Indonesia. Indonesian players won both men's and women's singles at the 1992 Olympics and an additional gold medal in men's doubles. Indonesia also won four of the five events at the 1994 World Championships. The 1996 Olympic Gold Medal men's and women's singles' champions were from Denmark and South Korea respectively. As mentioned earlier, the United States won the gold metal at the 2005 World Championships in Anaheim, California. Tony Gunawan and Howard Bach won the first ever World Individual Championship for the United States. Reports indicate approximately 50,000 active badminton players in the United States. Badminton is currently the number one sport in Great Britain. The total number of registered badminton players in England is reportedly almost two million. The Republic of China claims to have over 10 million badminton players. The WBF increased to 156 member nations in January, 2007. Prize money for the World Super Series and Final for 2007 will exceed three million dollars. The future for both competitive and recreational badminton seems very bright.

If you are interested in additional information, a complete listing of videos and instructional aids, the National Coaching Certification Program or in becoming more involved in competitive badminton by joining USA Badminton and taking advantage of its membership benefits, contact:

USA Badminton
One Olympic Plaza
Colorado Springs, Colorado 80909
Tel: (719) 866-4808   FAX: (719) 866-4507
E-mail: usab@usabadminton.org
Webside: http://www.usabadminton.org.

Equipment

2

Badminton is a game played with rackets and shuttlecocks on a court divided by a net. The cost and quality of badminton equipment varies greatly. The two premier badminton supply companies in the United States are:

> Louisville Badminton Supply
> 1313 Lyndon Lane, Suite 103
> Louisville, KY 40222
> (502) 426-3219

> San Diego Badminton Supply
> 2571 S. Coast highway 101
> Cardiff by the Sea, CA 92007
> (760) 633-1996 or in the U.S. 1-888-BADMINTON

RACKETS

Rackets vary greatly in price as they do in quality and design. A top grade racket, whether boron, carbon, graphite, metal or some other composite, may range in cost from 50 to 150 dollars for the frame alone. Beginners and even intermediate level players do not need to purchase the most expensive racket. A good medium priced racket is suggested as the place to start. One should test the feel of a new racket by swinging it freely in the store. It is a good idea to hit with several types of rackets. If possible, borrow one from a friend. Some sporting goods stores

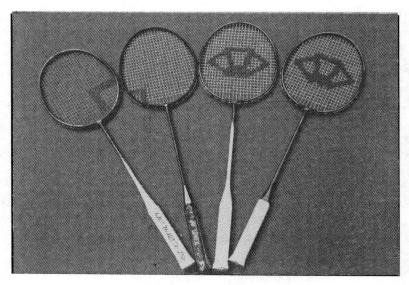

Figure 2-1. Rackets

have demonstration rackets that they will allow you to try out. Compare and choose the racket that feels most comfortable to you.

The lightness of the badminton racket enables it to be used effectively and to be manipulated at great speed without loss of control. Though rackets vary, most weigh approximately four ounces or less. The newer, lighter rackets of boron/carbon and graphite are often one piece in design and can be made of varying degrees of stiffness. There are also new wide-body badminton racket frames similar in concept and design to the latest in tennis rackets. These space-age materials allow for an extremely strong, yet very light racket. Some of these provide a wider, thinner head shape for less air resistance and less torque. **Carlton** and **Yonex** are still the leaders in terms of quality and selection. However, numerous other brand names, such as,

Blacknight, HL International and **ProKennex** are comparable in quality and price. A well balanced racket with its weight equivalent to the strength and ability of the player is an important consideration when purchasing this equipment. Figure 2-1 shows several quality rackets from various manufacturers.

Racket handles range from 3 1/2 to 3 7/8 inches in circumference. Above all else, the racket grip size should feel comfortable to the user. Most quality rackets come with a perforated, leather grip which provides durability and a consistent grip. Terricloth, foam or rubber grip wraps, tapes and/or gauzes may also be added to cushion the hand and to prevent the racket from slipping in the hand. Most rackets come with racket head covers or complete racket covers to protect the racket when not in use.

STRINGS

Strings are usually gut, nylon or synthetic. Gut is more resilient, pliable, and offers greater "touch," but is generally more costly ($20-30) and less durable due primarily to changes in the weather. Gut frays quickly, especially in wet weather and the string tension is affected greatly by changes in humidity. Synthetic strings are multifilament and offer most of the positive attributes of regular gut but are less affected by humidity and are much more durable. It is also slightly less expensive (15-25). Synthetics all have a core which is either straight, twisted or braided. A newer version also has a titanium coating.

Nylon is a monofilament and is significantly less expensive ($10-20), more durable, and is often strung tighter than gut. Nylon, gut and synthetic strings all come in various guages or thicknesses. Most quality badminton strings run from 18 to 21 guage or from 0.66 to 0.85 millimeters in thickness. The thinner gauges seem to offer slightly less air resistance. Most rackets are strung from 15 to 22 pounds per square inch tension. Research indicates that the more tightly strung racket offers greater control while the more loosely strung racket provides more power.

Since nylon and synthetic gut outlast gut and are immune to moisture and humidity changes, they seem more practical for the average player.

SHUTTLECOCKS

Shuttlecocks, shuttles or "birds" come in basically three varieties: plastic, nylon, or feather. Plastic shuttles are limited to recreational use, primarily out of doors. Because they are generally heavier, they are less affected by the wind. The nylon type is most often used in school or college badminton classes. It is much more consistent than the plastic variety as well as more durable and less expensive than feather shuttles.

Nylon and feathered birds come in designated speeds. **Carlton** tournament nylon birds, for example, have three speeds each indicated by the color of the band around the nylon base or tip. The RED band indicates fast, the BLUE is medium speed, and the GREEN is slow. The goose feathered shuttlecock has small pieces of lead shot in the cork tip as ballast to determine the speed of its flight. These feathered shuttlecocks are designated by weight as to their speed. Since elevation in relation to sea level greatly determines the amount of air resistance, a shuttle used near sea level must be heavier than one used at altitude. For example, in a city like Houston near the ocean, a 76-78 pound grain shuttle is desired. While badminton play in Mexico City, 7500 feet above sea level, requires a much lighter shuttle of approximately 43 grains. The proper procedure for testing the shuttle prior to tournament play is discussed in detail in Chapter 5.

The feathered shuttlecock is considered primarily for tournament play. It has a truer flight and provides for greater control on sliced or cut returns as well as tight play at the net. This feathered shuttle typically has from 16-18 goose feathers stitched and glued together to form the skirt. These feathers are secured into a cork base which is then covered with a thin, leather cover and wrapped with a small piece of green tape. Several high quality feathered shuttles are available, most notable, **Sportcraft** (Carlton), **Yonex, HL International** and **Reinforced Shuttlecocks Limited** (RSL).

However, in recent years, the tournament nylon shuttle has been significantly improved. Several versions now available with a cork base and nylon skirt which offers the advantage of durability and similar flight characteristics to the feathered shuttle. Notable examples are the **Yonex Mavis 300/350** and the **HL International** tournament nylon shuttlecocks. In addition to the traditional white shuttle, these newer, nylon shuttles also come in an optic, yellow for contrast and better visibility. Plastic birds range from $4-5 per dozen, nylon shuttles from $12-13 per dozen, and top quality, feathered shuttlecocks from $18-20 per dozen.

DRESS

Traditional badminton dress is in all white, primarily because white reflects heat better than darker colors and is cooler. The recent emphasis of television on clothing styles and the use of colors for contrast has started a trend away from the traditional white. However, light or pastel colors are most recommended along with white.

Badminton clothing generally consists of shorts, shirt, tennis shoes (or some other acceptable hardwood court shoes) and socks, and possibly a warm-up suit, sweater, or jacket. Many players wear nylon, cycling shorts or a cotton pant liner under their shorts for support and comfort. A blouse and skirt or a tennis dress may be preferred by some women. In addition, headbands, wristbands and towels may be needed to help keep perspiration from the eyes and the hands. A soft, leather glove is often used to provide a better grip and cushion the hand.

COURTS

The official rules of badminton standardize the dimensions of the badminton court and the height of the net. The badminton court for singles is 44 feet long and 17 feet wide thus it is termed to be long and narrow. The court for doubles is 44 feet long and

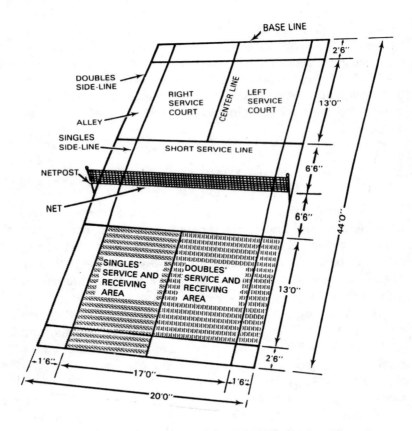

Figure 2-2. Badminton Court Areas and Lines

20 feet wide. Figure 2-2 illustrates the court areas and lines. The net should be five feet and one inch high at the net poles with it sloping to five feet at the top center of the net.

There is no official or standardized surface for badminton courts. A court may be indoors or outdoors; it may be concrete, asphalt, clay, grass, synthetic, or wood. However, most competitive badminton is played indoors and due to the existing hardwood floors available in most college and school gymnasiums, wood is the most often used surface. Several synthetic carpets or rubberized court surfaces are available commercially, such as, **Supreme Court**, **Yonex** and **Boltex**.

Fundamentals 3

In badminton, the lighter racket makes it possible for wrist action initiated by forearm rotation to be used effectively and therefore, the racket can be manipulated at a greater speed. In addition to the light racket, the lighter object (shuttle) to be contacted makes greater use of the wrist possible without loss of control. The racket head may be moving at a terrific rate of speed as it is thrown out to meet the shuttle. This indicates that a firm grip is needed at the instant contact is made. However, it is essential not to grip the racket tightly. Ideally, the grip in badminton should provide for flexible and effortless movement of the wrist.

THE FOREHAND GRIP

The forehand grip is used when hitting shots on the dominant side of the body which in most cases is the right side. This grip is sometimes referred to as either the "handshake" or "pistol" grip. Slide the racket into the hand as if "shaking hands" with it. The right forefinger is slightly spread apart from the other fingers providing the trigger finger effect as in holding a pistol. The racket should be lying across the palm and fingers with the thumb and index finger forming a V on top of the racket handle. If the racket is perpendicular to the floor, you are holding the racket correctly for the forehand. It is almost identical to the Eastern forehand grip in tennis.

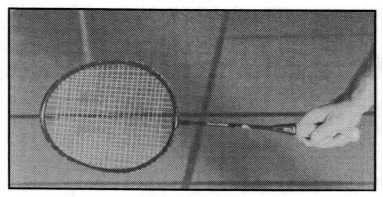

Figure 3-1. Forehand Grip

Figure 3-2. Backhand Grip

THE BACKHAND GRIP

The backhand grip is used when hitting shots on the non-dominant or left side of the body in most cases. For the backhand, the only change from the forehand is that the thumb is straight up and down on the top, left-hand bevel of the handle instead of wrapped around it. The advantage of this grip is that it enables you to hit all shots without actually changing your grip.

The thumb-up grip provides added support and leverage in all backhand strokes. While some players believe you can change your grip by merely loosening your hold on the racket, turning it slightly and assuming the new hold, time is of the essence. The word "time" as used in badminton play refers to split seconds. When you do have more time, such as on a high, deep clear to your backhand, a slight turn to the left from your forehand grip with the knuckle of the forefinger on the top plate of the handle and the thumb placed diagonally across and up the back of the handle provides slightly more power. However, this grip resembles the Eastern Backhand grip in tennis and effectively locks the wrist. As long as the shuttle is contacted in front of the body, this presents no problem. But in badminton, the shuttle often is hit deep to the backhand corner and one must actually hit the shuttle when it is past you or behind you. When this happens, the Eastern Backhand grip becomes a great liability. The previously recommended backhand grip which is similar to the forehand grip allows much greater wrist action. It permits the face of the racket to direct the shuttle into the opponent's court even when one's back is to the net and the shuttle is significantly behind you.

THE BASIC STROKES

The four basic shots in badminton are the clear, the smash, the drop shot, and the drive. All of these can be hit on the forehand or the backhand. The clear can be hit either overhand or underhand .

The overhead strokes will usually be made from the back half of your court. As the shuttle is hit up to your side, turn your body so that you r feet are perpendicular to the net. If the shuttle is hit to your forehand, your left shoulder should be pointing to the net. If it is to your backhand, your right shoulder should be towards the net. Shift your weight to the back foot, and, if necessary, skip backward until you are slightly behind the dropping shuttle. This is your hitting stance. The shuttle should be con-

Fundamentals

FOREHAND OVERHAND MOTION

Figure 3-3. Hitting Stance

Figure 3-4. Upward Extension to Contact

Figure 3-5. Forward Swing

Figure 3-6. Follow-through

BACKHAND OVERHAND MOTION

Figure 3-7. Hitting Stance

Figure 3-8. Forward Swing

Figure 3-9. Contact

Figure 3-10. Follow-through

tacted at the highest possible point and in front of the body. The angle that the shuttle will travel is dependent upon the angle of the face of the racket when contact is made. On the overhead returns, the follow through is down and in line with the flight of the shuttle. The ideal situation for all returns requires getting in position behind the bird, rotating the forearm, and shifting your weight in the direction of the hit.

Following will be a brief discussion of the mechanics of all overhead strokes in badminton. As you move to the oncoming shuttle, the racket arm is raised, the wrist is cocked, and the racket is placed downward. On the forehand, the racket is placed behind the head with the racket head down between the shoulder blades. On the backhand, the arm is lifted from the shoulder with the forearm parallel to the floor and the racket head pointed downward. When the stroke is made, several things occur very rapidly: (1) there is an upward extension of the arm led by the elbow, and vigorous rotation of the forearm and wrist; (2) at contact, the rapid rotation of the forearm has provided most of the power with the wrist being allowed to uncock naturally so that the arm is fully extended; and (3) the racket head follows through downward and in line with the return.

Actually the forehand and backhand overhead strokes are mirror images of one another. The extension of the arm at the elbow and vigorous forearm rotation provide the majority of the power for all overhead strokes. Forearm pronation occurs on the forehand stroke and forearm supination occurs on the backhand stroke. Classical wrist flexion or "wrist snap" occurs very little, if at all. The proper technique allows the wrist to uncock naturally with the racket following through in the direction of the return. For example, if one were to film the overhead forehand stroke and then project the film in reverse, it would very much resemble the overhead backhand stroke. Anatomically, the forearm works or rotates only in those two ways. Notice the similarities of the arm and wrist action as depicted by the sequence photographs on pages 20 and 21.

The forehand overhead motion can be compared to throwing a ball, as the mechanics are almost identical. Good performance is denoted by the general heading of a "throwing motion." Throwing motion is defined as the properly timed coordination of accelerations and decelerations of all body segments in a sequence of action from the left foot to the right hand that produces maximum absolute velocity of the right hand and in turn the racket. These same mechanics are used in the overhead strokes of the clear, smash, and drop. Attempt to make all three stokes look the same in order to make your shots deceptive. Then your opponent cannot tell which stroke you are playing until the shuttle has been contacted. The difference between these three strokes lies in: (1) point of contact between shuttle and racket and thus the angle at which the shuttle leaves the racket; and (2) the speed of racket at contact which determines the speed of the returning shuttle. Attempt to make the backswing, the forward swing (particularly the upper body turn) and the follow-through of all the overhead strokes as similar as possible. This will produce the most deception and make the direction of the return difficult to read.

Clear

The clear is a high shot to the back of the court. It may be hit either overhand or underhand, on the backhand or the forehand. The underhand clear is identical to the high, long serve and will be discussed in the section on serves.

To execute a good overhand clear, take the proper grip and move to a place where one is in the correct relationship to the shuttle. As one moves to position behind the shuttle, he should pivot at the waist and turn the shoulders sideways to the net. In badminton, the racket is literally thrown at the shuttle. The contact point is in front of the player. The best position is behind and in line with the shuttle. Overheads should be taken at the highest possible point of contact.

Always hit the shuttle as soon as possible so that the opponent will have less time to get to the shots. Meet the shuttle with a flat racket without cutting or slicing the bird. Since the shuttle should go high and deep, the racket will swing forward and up with the hand leading, then the follow-through will simply follow the shuttle. The racket should finish pointing down because of the forearm rotation. The shuttle is hit high enough so that at a point above the back boundary line, it loses speed and falls straight down. A shuttle falling perpendicular to the floor is the most difficult to play.

The high, deep clear is used primarily to gain time to return to the center position in the court. Another value of the high, deep clear is in its use in combination with the dropshot to run the opponent and make him defend all four corners of the court. Depth and height are extremely important in order to force the opponent as deep as possible.

Smash

The smash is a shot hit downward with force used to "put away" any shuttle hit upward and short. The smash should simulate a clear or a drop. Use the same grip, footwork, body position, and backswing as with the clear and the drop, and the opponent will not anticipate the return. The smash differs from the clear and the drop shot in that it can only be hit from an overhead position. Move to a position behind the shuttle as quickly as possible. Balance is needed to achieve maximum power from the shoulders, arms and wrist. The racket head must be moving at a rapid rate as it goes out to meet the shuttle. Contact the shuttle at the highest possible point and follow-through down and in line with the flight of the shuttle. One should try to get his timing and downward angle correct before attempting to get excessive speed.

The racket face should be angled downward at contact to make the shuttle travel downward. Remember that the farther away from the net, the less angle to the floor you can get. Also, the farther from the net when smashing, the less speed the smash will have when it reaches the other side of the net.

Drop Shot

The drop shot is hit just over the net so that the shuttle "drops" directly down towards the floor. To execute it, use exactly the same grip, footwork, body position, and backswing described for the overhead smash. The intention should be to suggest that a clear or a smash is about to be hit. The difference lies in racket speed. The shuttle is stroked or blocked rather than patted. The shuttle should be contacted farther in front of the body than the clear and directed downward. The face of the racket is tilted at the angle the shuttle is to take.

The outstanding characteristic of a good drop shot is deception. If the drop shot is deceptive enough, it can be an outright winner.

The worst characteristic of the drop shot is its slow flight. Anything moving slowly, unfortunately, gives the opponent time. The drop must be extremely accurate, then to be effective in relation to your position and your opponent's position on the court.

Drive

The drive is a flat stroke that sends the shuttle in a horizontal path across the net. The forehand drive is played on the dominant side of the body and is similar to the baseball sidearm throw. Because the drive is generally taken to the right or left of center court and between shoulder and knee height, the hitting stance will be slightly different from that of the three previous strokes. Badminton footwork stresses moving to the shuttle by shuffling or sliding the feet into position. Reach for the shuttle with the dominant arm and leg, crossing your feet over only on the backhand, not the forehand. The backhand drive seems to be the best place to begin to learn the backhand. The overhead backhand requires a great deal of timing to insure that the shuttle is contacted properly and that the racket is at its maximum speed when contact is made. While in the backswing position, the

FOREHAND DRIVE

Figure 3-11. Hitting Stance

Figure 3-12. Forward Swing

Figure 3-13. Contact

Figure 3-14. Follow-through

BACKHAND DRIVE

Figure 3-15. Hitting Stance

Figure 3-16. Forward Swing

Figure 3-17. Contact

Figure 3-18. Follow-through

dominant arm is bent with the racket face parallel to the ground, as shown in Figure 3-15. As the arm and racket swing forward, the right-handed individual should transfer body weight from the left foot to the right foot, rolling the forearm over and contacting the shuttle as the wrist uncocks. This forearm rotation causes the racket face to be flat in the direction that the shuttle is to travel, as shown in Figure 3-17. The arm straightens out at the point of contact. Contact should be made well away from the body so that the swing is not restricted. The racket follows through in the direction of the flight of the shuttle.

Hard hit, deep drives or slower paced midcourt drives can be played diagonally cross court or straight ahead parallel to the sidelines. If the shuttle is hit below knee level with great speed, it will be traveling up as it goes over the net and will continue to rise as it carries into the other court giving the advantage to your opponent. A less powerful drive that reaches its peak at the net and descends from there to midcourt is particularly valuable in doubles when you do not want to lift the shuttle up to your opponent. However, this shot should be directed down the sidelines in the alleys.

SERVES

In serving, the shuttle must not be struck higher than the waist and the shaft of the racket must be pointing in a downward direction with the entire racket head discernibly below the server's racket hand.

The underhand serve puts the bird in play at the beginning of each rally. It is probably the most important single stroke. Without an adequate serve, it is very difficult to score consistently. In addition, the beginning player should learn this stroke immediately for practice purposes. It can be used to set up your partner for practicing many strokes or for drills.

High-Long Serve

The high, long serve is used most often in singles play. It very closely resembles the forehand, underhand clear. The shuttle should be hit high and deep enough to cause it to turn over and fall in a perpendicular path as close to the back boundary line as possible. This lessens the effectiveness of a smash and results in a serve which is more difficult to time and hit solidly. The server should stand close to the center line and from three to five feet behind the short service line. The serving stance should be a comfortable one with the feet staggered in a stride position with the nondominant foot forward. The shuttle should be held at its base between the forefinger and thumb. The arm and hand holding the bird are extended out in front of the body at chest level. The racket arm is extended in a backswing position with the forearm and wrist in a cocked position. This position is also taken in preparing for the forehand, underhand clear. As the shuttle drops, the weight shifts from the back foot to the forward foot and the arm swings down to contact the shuttle at knee level. Forearm rotation and wrist action again provide the power. The follow-through is upward in line with the flight of the shuttle and finishing over the opposite shoulder.

Short-Low Serve

The short, low serve is the basic doubles serve, although it is often used in singles also. The low serve is more effective because the doubles service court is 30 inches shorter than singles and 18 inches wider. A long serve must be hit shorter in order to be good and therefore can be more easily smashed by your opponent. The shuttle should be directed to the junction of the center line and the short service line (the T) which eliminates the amount of angle available for your opponent's return. It also will hopefully force the receiver to hit upward to your partner waiting to smash the return.

HIGH, LONG SERVE/UNDERHAND CLEAR

**Figure 3-19. Backswing
to Cocked Position**

**Figure 3-20. Forward Swing
to Contact**

Figure 3-21. Follow-through

FOREHAND SHORT SERVE

**Figure 3-22. Backswing
to Cocked Position**

**Figure 3-23. Foreward Swing
to Contact**

Figure 3-24. Follow-through

BACKHAND SHORT SERVE

Figure 3-25. Ready Position
and Backswing

Figure 3-26. Contact

Figure 3-27. Follow-through

The short serve should be hit with the same preparation as the long serve, but the bird is guided low over the net to land just inside the service court. The arm makes the same backswing and forward motion, but there is little or no wrist action as the bird is "pushed" over the net rather than hit.

Another variation of this serve is a backhand short serve. Introduced by Asiatic players and currently used by many Americans, the backhand serve is hit in front of the server's body. Advantages of the backhand short serve include a shorter distance for the shuttle to travel, thus getting across the net and to the receiver sooner, and a blending of the bird with the server's body and clothing providing a form of camouflage. The bird is again guided or pushed over the net with the backhand motion. A flick serve can also be hit from this backhand position very effectively.

FLIGHT PATTERNS OF THE SHUTTLE

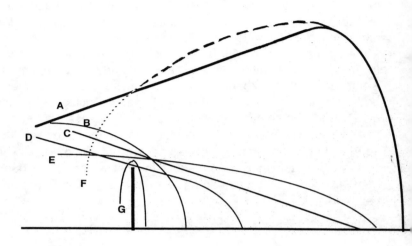

A.   Overhead Clear
B.   Overhead Drop Shot
C.   Overhead Smash
D.   Fast Drop Shot
E.   Drive
F.   Underhand Clear
G.   Hairpin Drop Shot

Figure 3-28. Various Shots

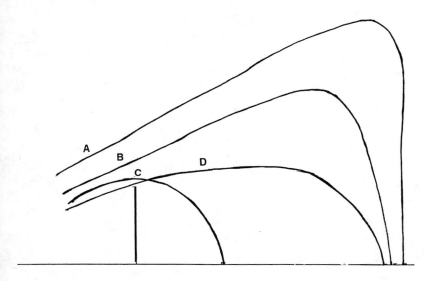

A. High Singles' Serve
B. Flick Serve
C. Low Doubles' Serve
D. Drive Serve

Figure 3-29. Serves

Footwork 4

Footwork in badminton is concerned with reaching the shuttle in as few steps as possible while maintaining good balance and body control. The beginning of good footwork is an alert waiting position.

THE READY POSITION

In the ready position, keep the feet spread shoulder width and bend the knees slightly with the weight on the balls of the

**Figure 4-1. Ready Position —
Front View**

**Figure 4-2. Ready Position —
Side View**

feet. The racket head should be held up, in front of the body slightly on the backhand side. From this position you are now ready to hit from either side as well as move forward or backward to attack or retrieve. It is very important to try to recover to this position after every shot so that you can move to the next shot. The best court position is center court at the short line which is equidistant from the four corners. This basic position on the court will enable you to reach most shots with less effort and in less time. From the ready position, you must be able to move quickly as soon as the direction of your opponent's return is determined. Most players vary the ready position some-what to meet their own style and needs. Some players stagger their feet slightly. This usually involves standing with the dominant foot slightly more forward. Small bouncy steps should be taken, shuffling or sliding into position to hit. Ideally, any shot may be intercepted in two or three steps.

RECEIVING THE SERVE

The waiting position for receiving the serve differs significantly from the normal ready position. The difference is primarily in the positioning of the feet and the racket. In order to be ready to move upward or backward and react to a long, short, flick or drive serve, the receiver must have the feet in a staggered or up and back position.

Figure 4-6 demonstrates the proper ready position to receive a serve in **singles'** play. Notice where the feet are in relation to the short service line and the center line. The forward foot should be 3-4 feet behind the short service line. Assuming the player is right handed, when receiving in the right court, one's overall position should be approximately one foot to the right of the center line. When receiving in the left court, one should position themselves 3-4 feet to the left of the center line. The racket is held up approximately chest or head high and in front of the dominant shoulder.

The proper ready position to receive serve in **doubles'** play is essentially the same position except, the receiver should position themselves as close to the short service line as they can comfortably get. Tournament level players almost always stand right at the short service line. Also, the racket is usually held slightly higher to react more quickly to a flick or drive serve.

Occasionally, usually in doubles, the server chooses to serve from a position nearer the doubles' sideline. This is done to create a better angle of attack to one's backhand particularly on a drive serve. The best way to counter attack this strategy is to open up your stance with the dominant foot in a forward stride position. This allows one to hit an around the head return on a drive serve much easier.

MOVEMENT ON THE COURT

Footwork is an essential fundamental skill of badminton. It gets you into the best possible position to execute your shots. The badminton shuttle rarely comes to you, thus you must move into position to hit the shuttle. Movement on the court is concerned with reaching the shuttle in as few steps as possible while maintaining good balance and body control. The ability to move to the shuttle quickly and effortlessly is important for every player to acquire. Yet, it is surprising how few players actually emphasize this part of their game. Americans especially seem to have less training in foot-related activities, such as soccer and ballet.

The purposes of any form of footwork are: (1) to get to the shuttle as soon as possible; (2) to maintain body balance at all times; and (3) to use as little energy as possible. Footwork should become habit and be a virtually automatic aspect of your game. But initially, it will take repetition and practice, along with some additional thought during play.

Actual movement on the court is discussed in two forms: the basic method and the "gravity method."

Basic Method

The basic method is used when less distance is to be traveled; for example, when the shuttle can be reached in approximately two steps and one does not have to move to the extreme corners of the court.

From the ready position, the nondominant foot is almost always the pivot foot and the dominant foot the leading one. Reaching for the shuttle with the dominant arm and leg saves time and the subsequent push-off on this leg aids in a swift recovery in changing direction. See Figures 4-3 and 4-4.

**Figure 4-3.
Lead with the
Dominant Foot**

Figure 4-4. Reach with the Dominant Hand

From center court, there are basically six directions you will need to move to. They are: (1) up, right to the net; (2) up, left to the net; (3) left to the sidelines; (4) backhand to the baseline; (5) forehand to the baseline; and (6) right to the sideline. In each case, as soon as the direction of the return is determined, pivot, then lead with the dominant foot taking a step-close or skipping action with the feet close to the floor. Cross your feet over only on the backhand, not on the forehand. Figures 4-5 and 4-6 illustrate the basic footwork used to intercept the oncoming shuttle. As the last step is made with the leading foot and the shuttle is contacted, you should push off with the lead foot propelling yourself back towards center court. The return to center will be a repeat of the steps taken to intercept the shuttle.

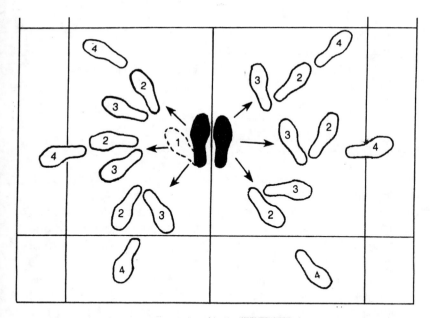

Figure 4-5. Basic footwork used to intercept oncoming shuttle for right-handed player.

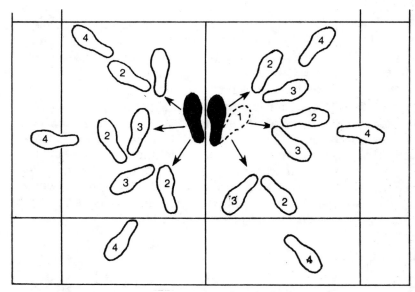

**Figure 4-6. Basic footwork used to intercept oncoming shuttle
for left-handed player.**

Gravity Method

If more speed is desired or a greater distance is to be covered, a
slight change that allows **gravity** to assist one in starting and/or
reversing one's movement is suggested. It is similar to the track
sprinter's start in which the base of support is removed and one
falls in the desired direction. From the ready position, instead of
the non-dominant foot simply pivoting, it is moved opposite of the
desired direction. Thus one falls in the desired direction with the
aid of gravity. This method seems to be most often used when
attempting to return to mid-court from a position near the net.
When traveling to the net, the dominant leg is normally leading
and is used to push-off and return to mid-court. However, if the
non-dominant foot is also brought forward and planted near the
dominant foot and one leans backward, the subsequent push-off
on both legs greatly assists gravity in changing direction. Actual

movement on the court is discussed in three categories: moving to the net, moving sideways, and moving to the back court.

Moving to the Net

From the ready position, a three-step pattern is sufficient for most players to reach the net. Whether moving up to the forehand or the backhand, the non-racket leg is pulled back and in from the ready stance allowing the body to fall forward. At the same time, the racket leg leads in the proper direction followed by the non racket leg in a step-close action. The third step is taken by the racket leg which is extended and planted in front of the body for the shot.

In order to divide the work load evenly between the two legs, pull the trailing leg up under the body and push back with both legs. Bringing both feet up straightens the body, actually causing it to fall back and make the return to center less tiring. The return in both cases is a three-step pattern: racket-leg, other leg, racket leg.

Moving Sideways

To the racket side, pull the non-racket leg in from the ready stance and propel the racket leg into a side step followed again by the non-racket leg in a step-close action. The third step is taken by the racket leg which is extended sideways in the direction of the oncoming shuttle.

To the other side, the non-racket leg is pulled in even farther and the racket leg is propelled into a cross-over step. Again the non-racket leg shuffles or slides in a step-close fashion and the racket leg follows with the third step in reaching for the shuttle.

The return to center court in both cases is the same three step pattern as before: racket-leg, other leg, racket-leg.

Moving Backwards

The three step pattern for moving backwards is very similar to moving sideways. However, whether forehand or backhand, the body must turn slightly in the direction to be moved.

As the body turns toward the forehand, the non-racket foot is moved in and slightly forward. Almost simultaneously, the racket leg reaches in the proper direction. The racket-leg leads while the non-racket leg catches up in a shuffling or step-close action. The racket leg is again propelled toward the direction of the oncoming shuttle. The racket leg is planted with the body sideways to the net and a normal overhead stroke is made.

For the backhand, the non-racket foot pulls in and allows the racket-leg to cross over and lead with the first step as the body turns in that direction. A shuffle step by the non-racket leg followed by a third step with the racket leg puts the body in position to execute the backhand overhead stroke.

As the shot is made, the non-racket leg is pulled back under the body causing it to fall forward and aiding in the return to center court. The return is again a three-step pattern.

SUMMARY

Both of the footwork methods are accepted and used to some extent by most experienced badminton players. They are quite similar except for the use of gravity in starting and changing direction. The gravity method also allows the non-racket leg to aid in changing direction. Ideally, one would probably use both methods during the course of a match. The basic method is sufficient when the shuttle is relatively close. But when it is necessary to lunge in close to the net or retreat for a deep return near the baseline, the gravity method is almost essential.

It is essential not to be moving when the opponent hits the shuttle. If it is not possible to get completely back to mid-court, stop where you are prior to the opponent hitting the shuttle. It will

Figure 4-7. Backswing Position   **Figure 4-8. Forward Swing to Contact**

Figure 4-9. Follow-through and Recovery

be easier to travel a slightly greater distance from a stand-still than trying to change direction while still moving. This is especially true even from the ready position. Do not guess or anticipate too soon. Wait until you are sure of the direction that the shuttle is traveling before moving.

The forehand and backhand drives provide an excellent opportunity to introduce footwork because the drive is generally taken to the right or left of center court and between shoulder and knee height. Thus, it stresses moving to the shuttle by shuffling or sliding the feet into position. From the ready position, as soon as the direction of the return is determined, pivot, reach with the dominant foot shuffling or taking a step-close or skipping action with the feet close to the floor. Cross the feet over on the backhand, but not the forehand. As the last step is taken, push off and propel yourself back towards center court. See Figures 4-7 through 4-9 which illustrate the forehand drive.

In the classroom situation, probably only a brief period will be spent on footwork due to limited time and space. However, repetition and practice to develop court speed and efficiency of movement are essential for the advanced player.

Badminton Scoring Simplified 5

Badminton rally scoring is similar to volleyball, in that, a point is scored on every rally. You decide who is serving first by the **toss**. This can be a coin toss, a spin of the racket or a toss/hit of the bird into the air to see towards whom it points when it lands. If you win the toss, you may choose to serve, to receive or choose the side of the court that you wish to start on. Whichever choice that you make, your opponent automatically gets to choose from the remaining options. Either opponent begins the game by serving from the right court with zero or "love-all." The court or side that you begin on is dependent on your score.

The serve is made diagonally across to your opponent. The feet of both the receiver and the server must be in the proper court and in contact with the floor until the serve is made by the server. When the receiver is ready, the server has only one attempt to put the shuttle into play with an underhand (below the waist) serve. The receiver can stand anywhere in the proper court, but must keep both feet in contact with the floor until the serve is delivered. If the receiver makes an attempt to hit the serve, he was considered to have been ready. After each rally or exchange, the server initiates the serve from the appropriate side depending on whether his score is odd or even. If his score is even, he is on the right; if it is an odd score, he is on the left. The score should always be announced prior to each service with the server's score given first. If a serve hits the top of the net and continues into the proper court, that serve is **not called a let**. This is a legal serve and play continues.

Games normally are played to twenty-one points in all events. A method of extending a tie game that was peculiar to badminton was the concept of **setting**. As of August 1, 2006, there is no longer an opportunity to set a game. However, if the score reaches **20-all**, the game may be extended until one player or team gains a two-point advantage. If the score reaches 29-all, the next point wins the game.

In summary, a rally is won (and a point is made) when the opponent(s):

— fails in attempting to return a legal serve;
— hits the shuttle outside of the proper boundary lines while serving;
— hits the shuttle into the net;
— hits the shuttle two or more times in returning the shuttle;
— touches the net with his body or racket while the shuttle is in play;
— lets the shuttle hit the floor inside the boundaries of the court;
— deliberately carries or catches the bird on the racket strings;
— does anything to hinder/interfere with your attempt to make a legal return;
— executes an illegal serve;
— reaches over the net to hit a return before the bird is on his side of the net;
— touches the bird with anything other than the racket during a rally;
— fails to keep both feet in contact with the floor while serving or receiving.

Any point that has to be replayed is called a **let**. These should occur very infrequently and are usually the result of some type of outside interference. A let might occur in the case of a shuttle, racket, some other object or person from an adjacent court entering your court and preventing the normal progression of a rally. Another example would be the disintegration or falling apart of the shuttle during play in which feathers actually separate from the cork base.

SINGLES RULES

The first serve is always made from the **right side**. This is because the server's score is zero, which is an even number. Anytime after the beginning of the game that the server's score is even, the service is delivered from the right side (2, 4, 6, 8, and so on). If a point is made, the server now serves from the left side, which is odd (1, 3, 5, 7, and so on). The score dictates which side of the court the serve is from.

The service court in singles' play is long and narrow. The side alley is out of bounds; the back alley is in bounds or good. The serve must carry past the short service line which is seven feet from the net and must not carry beyond the back boundary line which is at the extreme rear of the court. The lines are considered part of the court and in bounds. A bird that lands on a line is considered to be inside the court and the rally is won.

DOUBLES RULES

Again, the first serve is always made from the **right side**. This is because the serving team's score is zero, which is an even number. In doubles, one partner starts on the right side and one partner starts on the left side. Anytime after the beginning of the game when a point is made, the server serves diagonally across to the other side. The score dictates which side of the court the serve is made.

In doubles, the first serve is always from the side dictated by your score. The team who serves gets only one serve. Like singles, all doubles games are played to 21 points. The option of setting no longer exists.

The service court in doubles' play is short and fat. The side alley is now in bounds and the back alley is out of bounds on the serve. However, once the bird is in play, the back alley is in play and a return that lands there is considered to be good and wins the rally. The serve must carry past the short service line which is seven feet from the net and must not carry beyond the inside doubles back line which is 18 inches inside of the back boundary line. The lines are considered part of the court and in bounds.

Laws of Badminton   6

The rules of scoring in badminton are respectfully referred to by the International Badminton Federation as the **Laws of Badminton**. These rules have changed very little over the past one hundred years. However in the late 1960s, the wood shot became a legal return. Prior to this time, any return that hit the frame or wood was considered illegal. Also during the late 1970's, it became popular to serve what was called a reverse or Sidek serve, in which the shuttle was held with the feathers downward and struck feathers first to produce an exaggerated sliced serve that literally looped over the net in a gyrating spiral. This type of serve was particularly effective at higher elevations, such as, in Mexico City. It was taught successfully for several years at the world class level and was perfected so well by the Sidek brothers from Indonesia that it was often referred to by their name. In the early 1980's, it too became illegal. The shuttle now is required to be struck tip or base first as described in **Rule 9.1.4** under the Laws of Badminton.

Two other significant rules were changed when the current Laws of Badminton were revised and adopted in 1990. It was stated that if a player has a chance of striking the shuttle in a downward direction when quite near the net, his opponent must not put up his racket near the net on the chance of the shuttle rebounding from it. This was deemed to be obstruction. This rule is no longer in the Laws of Badminton. One of the more significant changes dealt with the server when attempting to hit the serve , misses the shuttle altogether. Prior to 1990, it was not a fault to swing and miss the shuttle while serving. Now **Rule 9.3** states that "it is a fault, if the server, in attempting to serve, misses the shuttle."

During the early 1990's, the IBF experimented with a new scoring system for singles, doubles and mixed doubles, with games to be played to nine points and the winner of the match being the player who wins three out of five games. There would be no setting or winning by two-point requirements. That attempt at changing the scoring was temporary and only slightly successful so the older method of keeping score was retained for the next decade. The BWF is now suggesting the elimination of the older method of keeping score with games to fifteen and to eleven along with the unique concept of setting. The former IBF at their annual general membership meeting voted to adopt the rally point system for all IBF sanctioned events. The USAB Board of Directors voted to adopt this policy for all USAB national ranking tournaments. Non-ranking tournaments that wish to be sanctioned by USAB would not be required to use rally points at this time. The rationale for this suggested change is to make the sport more marketable to spectators and television alike, as well as, to improve its acceptance and understanding by the general population. Preliminary observations seem to indicate that matches may be reduced by as much as 25%. The rally scoring system requires players to be more alert and to score quickly in these abbreviated games. Athletes will be required to adapt to a new strategy for winning matches. It is suggested that spectators will also benefit from this exciting and potentially pressure-packed format.

The **Simplified New Rally Points Scoring System** follows as amended and adopted by the WBF and USAB effective, August 2006. The original **Laws of Badminton** are also included in their entirety as amended and adopted as of August 1, 2002. They are reprinted by permission.

SIMPLIFIED NEW RALLY POINTS SCORING SYSTEM

Scoring System

- A match consists of the best of three games of 21 points.
- The side winning a rally adds a point to its score.
- At 20 all, the side which gains a 2-point lead first, wins that game.
- At 29-all, the side scoring the 30th point, wins that game.
- The side winning a game serves first in the next game.

Intervals and Change of Ends

- When the leading score reaches 11 points, players have a 60-second interval
- A 2-minute interval between eachgame is allowed.
- In the third game, players change ends when a side scores 11 points.

Singles

- At the beginning of the game and when the score is even, the server serves from the right service court. When it is odd, the server serves from the left service court.
- If the server wins a rally, the server scores a point and then serves again from alternate service court.
- If the receiver wins a rally, the receiver scores a point and becomes the new server.

Doubles

- There is only one serve in doubles (see attached diagram). The service passes consecutively to the players as shown in the attached diagram.

- At the beginning of the game and when the score is even, the server serves from the right court. When it is odd, the server serves from the left court.

- If the serving side wins a rally, the serving side scores a point and the same server serves again from the alternate service court.

- If the receiving side wins a rally, the receiving side scores a point. The receiving side becomes the new serving side.

- The player of the receiving side who served last stays in the same service court from where he served last. The reverse pattern applies to the receiver's partner.

- The players do not change their respective service courts until they win a point when their side is serving.

- If players commit an error in the service court, the error is corrected when the mistake is discovered.

LAWS OF BADMINTON
(AS OF AUGUST 1, 2002)

1.   COURT AND COURT EQUIPMENT

1.1   The court shall be a rectangle and laid out as shown in Diagram A.

1.2   The lines shall be easily distinguishable and preferably be colored white or yellow.

1.3   All lines form part of the area which they define.

1.4   The posts shall be 5′1″ in height from the surface of the court and shall remain vertical when the net is strained as provided in Law 1.10.

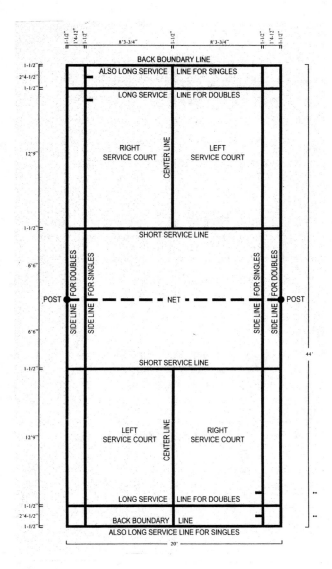

Diagram A. Court which can be used for singles or doubles play.

1.5   The posts shall be placed on the doubles side lines as in Diagram A, irrespective of whether singles or doubles is being played.

1.6   The net shall be made of fine cord of dark color and even thickness with a mesh of not less than 5/8″ and not more than 3/4″.

1.7   The net shall be 2′6″ in depth and at least 20′ wide.

1.8   The top of the net shall be edged with a 3″ white cloth tape doubled over a cord or cable running through the tape. This tape must rest upon the cord or cable.

1.9   The cord or cable shall be stretched firmly, flush with the top of the posts.

1.10   The top of the net from the surface of the court shall be 5′ at the center of the court and 5′1″ over the side lines for doubles.

1.11   There shall be no gaps between the ends of the net and the posts. If necessary, the full depth of the net should be tired at the ends.

2.   SHUTTLE

2.1   The shuttle may be made from natural and/or synthetic materials. From whatever mater the shuttle is made, the flight characteristics generally should be similar to those produced by a natural feathered shuttle with a cork base covered by a thin layer of leather.

2.2   The shuttle shall have 16 feathers fixed in the base.

2.3   The feathers shall be measured from the tip to the top of the base and each shuttle shall be of the same length. This length can be between 2-1/2″ and 2-3/4″.

2.4   The tips of the feathers shall lie on a circle with a diameter from 2-1/4″ to 2-5/8″.

2.5   The feathers shall be fastened firmly with thread or other suitable material.

2.6   The base shall be 1″ to 1-1/8″ in diameter and rounded on the bottom.

2.7   The shuttle shall weigh from 4.74 to 5.50 grams.

2.8   Non-Feathered Shuttle

   2.81   The skirt, or simulation of feathers in synthetic materials, replaces natural feathers.

   2.8.2   The base is described in Law 2.6.

   2.8.3   Measurements and weight shall be as in Laws 2.3, 2.4 and 2.7. However, because of the difference in the specific gravity and other properties of synthetic materials in comparison with feathers, a variation of up to 10 percent is acceptable.

2.9   Subject to there being no variation in the design, speed and flight of the shuttle, modifications in the above specifications may be made with the approval of the Member Association concerned:

   2.9.1   in places where atmostpheric conditions due to either altitude or climate make the standard shuttle unsuitable

   2.9.2   if special circumstances exist which made it otherwise necessary in the interests of the game

3.   TESTING A SHUTTLE FOR SPEED

3.1   To test a shuttle, use a full underhand stroke which makes contact with the shuttle over the back boundary line. The shuttle shall be hit at an upward angle and in a direction parallel to the side lines.

3.2   A shuttle of correct speed will land not less than 1'9" and not more than 3'3" short of the other back boundary line as in Diagram B.

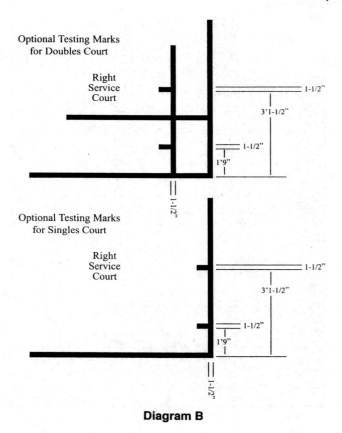

Diagram B

4.   RACKET

4.1   The parts of a racket are described in Laws 4.1.1 to 4.1.7 and are illustrated in Diagram C.

  4.1.1   The main racket parts are called the handle, the stringed area, the head, the shaft, and throat and the frame.

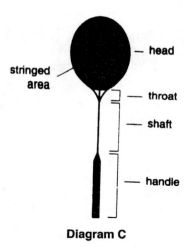

stringed area

— head

— throat

— shaft

— handle

Diagram C

4.1.2   The handle is the part of the racket intended to be gripped by the player.

4.1.3   The stringed area is the part of the racket with which it is intended the player hits the shuttle.

4.1.4   The head bounds the stringed area.

4.1.5   The shaft connects the handle to the head (subject to Law 4.1.6).

4.1.6   The throat (if present) connects the shaft to the head.

4.1.7   The frame is the name given to the head, throat, shaft and handle taken together.

4.2   The frame of the racket shall not exceed 2′2-3/4″ in overall length and 9″ in overall width.

4.3   Stringed area

4.3.1   The stringed area shall be flat and consist of a pattern of crossed strings either alternately interlaced or bonded where they cross. The stringing pattern shall be generally uniform and, in particular, not less dense in the center than in any other area.

4.3.2　The stringed area shall not exceed 11″ in overall length and 8-5/8″ in overall width. However, the strings may extend into an area which otherwise would be the throat, provided that the width of the extended stringed area does not exceed 1′1/8″ and provided that the overall length of the stringed area does not then exceed 1′1″.

4.4　The racket:

4.4.1　Shall be free of attached objects and protrusions, other than those used solely and specifically to limit or prevent wear and tear, or vibration, or to distribute weight, or to secure the handle by cord to the player's hand, and which are reasonable in size and placement for such purposes; and

4.4.2　Shall be free of any device which makes it possible for a player to change materially and shape of the racket.

5.　EQUIPMENT COMPLIANCE

The International Badminton Federation shall rule on any question of whether any racket, shuttle or equipment or any prototype used in the playing of badminton complies with the specifications. Such ruling may be undertaken on the Federation's initiative or upon application by any party with a bona fide interest therein, including any player, equipment manufacturer or Member Association or member thereof.

6.　TOSS

6.1　Before play commences, a toss shall be conducted and the side winning the toss shall exercise the choice in either Law 6.11 or Law 6.12.

6.1.1　To serve or receive first.

6.1.2　To start play at one end of the court or the other.

6.2　The side losing the toss shall then exercise the remaining choice.

7. SCORING

7.1   A match shall consist of the best of three games unless, otherwise arranged.

7.2   In doubles and men's singles a game is won by the first side to score 15 points, except as provided in Law 7.4.

7.3   In ladies' singles a game is won by the first side to score 11 points, except as provided in Law 7.4

7.4   If the score becomes 14-all(10-all in ladies' singles), the side which first scored 14 (10) shall exercise the choice in Law 7.4.1 or 7.4.2;

    7.4.1   To continue the game to 15 (11) points, i.e., not to "set" the game, or

    7.4..2   To "set" the game to 17 (13) points.

7.5   The side winning a game serves first in the next game.

7.6   Only the serving end can add a point to its score (see Law 10.3 or 11.4)

8. CHANGE OF ENDS

8.1   Players shall change ends:

    8.1.1   At the end of the first game;

    8.1.2   Prior to the beginning of the third game (if any); and

    8.1.3   In the third game, or in a match of one game, when the leading score reaches:

        — 6 in a game of 11 points; or

        — 8 in a game of 15 points.

8.2   if players omit to change ends as indicated in Law 8.1, they shall do so as soon as the mistake is discovered and the shuttle is not in play. The existing score shall stand.

9.   SERVICE

9.1   In a correct service:

   9.1.1   Neither side shall cause undue delay to the delivery of the service once server and receiver have taken up their respective positions;

   9.1.2   The server and receiver shall stand within diagonally opposite service courts without touching he boundary lines of these service courts;

   9.1.3   Some part of both feet of the server and receiver must remain in contact with the surface of the court in a stationary position from the start of the service until the service is delivered (Law 9.6);

   9.1.4   The server's racket shall initially hit the base of the shuttle;

   9.1.5   The whole of shuttle shall be below the server's waist at the instant of being hit by the server's racket;

   9.1.6   The shaft of he server's racket at the instant of hitting the shuttle shall be pointing in a downward direction to such an extent that the whole of he head of the racket is discernibly below the whole of the server's hand holding the racket as in Diagram D.

   9.1.7   The movement of the server's racket must continue forwards after the start of the service (Law 9.4) until the service is delivered; and

   9.1.8   The flight of the shuttle shall be upwards from the server's racket to pass over the net so that, if not intercepted, it falls in the receiver's service court (ie on or within the boundary lines).

9.2   If a service is not correct by virtue of any of Laws 9.1.1 to 9.1.8, it shall be a 'fault' (Law 13) by the offending side.

9.3   It is a 'fault' if the server, it attempting to serve, misses the shuttle.

9.4   Once the players have taken their positions, the first forward movement of the server's racket head is the start of the service.

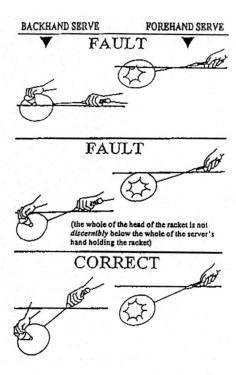

Diagram D. Positions of the racket and of the server's hand holding it at the instant of striking the shuttle.

9.5. The server shall not serve before the receiver is ready but the receiver shall be considered to have been ready if a return of service is attempted.

9.6 Once the service is started (Law 9.4), it is delivered when the shuttle is hit by the server's racket or, in attempting to serve, the server misses the shuttle.

9.7 In doubles, he partners may take up any positions which to not unsight the opposing server or receiver.

10.   SINGLES

10.1   Serving and receiving courts

 10.1.1   The players shall serve from, and receive in, their respective right service courts when the server has not scored or has scored an even number of points in that game.

 10.1.2   The players shall serve from, and receive in, their respective left serve courts when the server has scored an odd number of points in that game.

10.2   The shuttle is hit alternately by the server and the receiver until a "fault" is made or the shuttle ceases to be in play.

10.3   Scoring and serving

 10.3.1   If the receiver makes a "fault" or the shuttle cases to be in play because it touches the surface of the court inside the receiver's court, the server scores a point. The server then serves again from the alternate service court.

 10.3.2   If the server makes a "fault" or the shuttle cases to be in play because it touches the surface of the court inside the server's court, the server loses the right to continue serving and the receiver then becomes the server, with no point scored by either player.

11.   DOUBLES

11.1   At the start of a game, and each time a side gains the right to serve, the service shall be delivered from the right service court.

11.2   Only the receiver shall return the service: should the shuttle touch or be hit by the receiver's partner, it shall be a 'fault' and the serving side scores a point.

11.3   Order of play and position on court

 11.3.1   After the service is returned, the shuttle may be hit by either player of the serving side and then by either player of the receiving side, and so on, until the shuttle cases to be in play.

11.3.2 After the service is returned, a player may hit the shuttle from any position on that player's side of the net.

11.4 Scoring and serving

11.4.1 if the receiving side makes a 'fault' or the shuttle cases to be in play because it touches the surface of the court inside the receiving side's court, the serving side scores a point and the server serves again.

11.4.2 If the serving side makes a 'fault' or the shuttle cases to be in play because it touches the surface of the court inside the serving side's court, the server loses the right to continue serving, with no point scored by either side.

11.5 Serving and receiving courts

11.5.1 The player who serves at the start of any game shall serve from, or receive in, the right service court when that player's side has not scored or has scored an even number of points in the game and the left service court when that player's side has scored an odd number of points in that game.

11.5.2 The player who receives at the start of any game shall receive in, or serve from, the right service court when that player's side has not scored or has scored an even number of points in that game and the left service court when that player's side has scored an odd number of points in that game.

11.5.3 The reverse pattern shall apply to the partners.

11.6 Service in any turn of serving shall be delivered from alternate service courts, except as provided in Laws 12 and 14.

11.7 In any game, the right to serve passes consecutively from the initial server to the initial receiver, then to the initial receiver's partner, then to the opponent who is due to serve from the right service court (Law 11.5), then to that player's partner, and so on.

11.8   No player shall serve out of turn, receive out of turn, or receive two consecutive services in the same game, except as provided in Laws 12 and 14.

11.9   Either player of the winning side may serve first in the next game, and either player of the losing side may receive.

12.   SERVICE COURT ERRORS

12.1   A service court error has been made when a player:

   12.1.1   Has served out of turn;

   12.1.2   Has served from the wrong service court; or

   12.1.3   Standing in the wrong service court, was prepared to receive the service and it has been delivered.

12.2   If a service court error is discovered after the next service has been delivered, the error shall not be corrected.

12.3   If a service court error is discovered before the next service is delivered:

   12.3.1   If both sides committed an error, it shall be a "let"

   12.3.2   If one side committed the error and won the rally, it shall be a "let"

   12.3.3   If one side committed the error and lost the rally, the error shall not be corrected

12.4   If there is a "let" because of a service court error, the rally is replayed with the error corrected.

12.5   If a service court error is not to be corrected, play in that game shall proceed without changing the players' new service courts (nor, when relevant, the new order of serving).

13.   FAULTS

It is a "fault":

13.1   If a service is not correct (Law 9.1) or if Law 9.3 or 11.2 applies:

13.2   If in play, the shuttle:

13.2.1 Lands outside the boundaries of the court (i.e. not on or within the boundary lines);

13.2.2. Passes through or under the net;

    13.3.3 Fails to pass the net;

    13.2.4 Touches the ceiling or side walls;

    13.2.5 Touches the person or dress of a player, or

    13.2.6 Touches any other object or person outside the immediate surroundings of the court;

    (Where necessary on account of the structure of the building, the local badminton authority may, subject to the right of veto of its Member Association, make bye-laws dealing with cases in which a shuttle touches an obstruction).

13.3 if, when in play, the initial point of contact with the shuttle is not on the striker's side of the net. (The striker may, however, follow the shuttle over the net with the racket in the course of a stroke);

13.4. If, when the shuttle is in play, a player:

    13.4.1 Touches the net or its supports with racket, person or dress;

    13.4.2 Invades an opponent's court over the net with racket or person except as permitted in Law 13.3.

    13.4.3 Invades an opponent's court under the net with racket or person such that an opponent is obstructed or distracted; or

    13.4.4 Obstructs an opponent, i.e. prevents an opponent from making a legal stroke where the shuttle is followed over the net.

13.5 If, in play, a player deliberately distracts an opponent by any action such as shouting or making gestures;

13.6 If, in play, the shuttle:

    13.6.1 Is caught and held on the racket and then slung during the execution of a stroke;

    13.6.2 Is hit twice in succession by the same player with two strokes;

13.6.3   Is hit by a player and the player's partner successively; or

13.6.4   Touches a player's racket and continues towards the back of that player's court;

13.7   If a player is guilty of flagrant, repeated or persistent offenses under Law 18.

13.8   If, on service, the shuttle is caught on the net and remains suspended on top or, on service, after passing over the net is caught in the net;

14. LETS

14.1   "Let" is called by the umpire, or by a player (if there is no umpire) to halt play.

14.2   A "let" may be given for any unforeseen or accidental occurrence.

14.3   If a shuttle is caught on the net and remains suspended on top or, after passing over the net, is caught in the net, it is a "let" except on service.

14.4   If during service, the receiver and server are both faulted at the same time, it shall be a "let."

14.5   If the server serves before the receiver is ready, it shall be a "let."

14.6   If during play, the shuttle disintegrates and the base completely separates from the rest of the shuttle, it shall be a "let."

14.7   If a line judge is unsighted and the umpire is unable to make a decision, it shall be a "let."

14.8   A "let" may occur following a service court error; see Law 12.3.

14.9   When a "let" occurs, the play since the last service shall not count and the player who served shall serve again, except where Law 14 is applicable.

15. SHUTTLE NOT IN PLAY

A shuttle is not in play when:

15.1 It strikes the net and remains attached there or suspended on top;

15.2 It strikes the net or post and starts to fall towards the surface of the court on the striker's side of the net;

15.3 It hits the surface of the court; or

15.4 A "fault" or "let" has occurred.

16. CONTINUOUS PLAY, MISCONDUCT, PENALTIES

16.1 Play shall be continuous from the first service until the match is concluded, except as allowed in Laws 16.2 and 16.3.

16.2 Intervals not exceeding 90 seconds between the first and second games, and not exceeding 5 minutes between the second and third games, are allowed in all matches in all of the following situations:

16.2.1 international competitive events;

16.2.2 IBF-sanctioned events; and

16.2.3 All other matches unless the Member Association has previously published a decision not to allow such intervals.

(In televised matches the Referee may decide before the match that intervals as in Law 16.2 are mandatory and of fixed duration.)

16.3 Suspension of play

16.3.1 When necessitated by circumstances not within the control of the players, the umpire may suspend play for such a period as the umpire may consider necessary

16.3.2 Under special circumstances the Referee may instruct the umpire to suspend play

16.3.3 If play is suspended, the existing score shall stand and play be resumed from that point.

16.4   Under no circumstances shall play be delayed to enable a player to recover strength or wind.

16.5   Advice and leaving the court

 16.5.1   Expert in the intervals provided in Laws 16.2 and 16.3, no player shall be permitted to receive advice during a match.

 16.5.2   Except during the five-minute interval described in Law 16.2, no player shall leave the court during a match without the umpire's permission.

16.6   The umpire shall be the sole judge of any suspension of play.

16.7   A player shall not:

 16.7.1   Deliberately cause delay in or suspension of play;

 16.7.2   Deliberately modify or damage the shuttle in order to change its speed or flight;

 16.7.3   Behave in an offensive manner; or

 16.7.4   Be guilty of misconduct not otherwise covered by the Laws of badminton.

16.8   The umpire shall administer any breach of Law 16.4, 16.5 or 16.7 by:

 16.8.1   Issuing a warning to the offending side;

 16.8.2   Faulting the offending side, if previously warned; or

 16.8.3   In cases of flagrant offense or persistent offenses, faulting the offending side and reporting the offending side immediately to the Referee, who shall have power to disqualify the offending side from the match.

17.   OFFICIALS AND APPEALS

17.1   The Referee is in overall charge of the tournament or event of which a match forms part.

17.2   The umpire, where appointed, is in charge of the match, the court and its immediate surrounds. The umpire shall report to the Referee.

17.3   The service judge shall call service faults made by the server should they occur (Law 9).

17.4   A line judge shall indicate whether a shuttle is "in" or "out" of the line(s) assigned.

17.5   An official's decision is final on all points of fact for which that official is responsible.

17.6   An umpire shall

17.6.1   Uphold and enforce the Laws of badminton and, especially, call a "fault" or "let" should either occur;

17.6.2   Give a decision on any appeal regarding a point of dispute, if made before the next service is delivered;

17.6.3   Ensure players and spectators are kept informed of the progress of the match;

17.6.4   Appoint or remove line judges or a service judge in consultation with the Referee;

17.6.5   Where another court official is not appointed, arrange for that official's duties to be carried out;

17.6.6   Where an appointed official is unsighted, carry out the official's duties or play a "let":

17.6.7   Record and report to the Referee all matters in relation to Law 16; and

17.6.8   Take to the Referee all unsatisfied appeals on questions of law only. (Such appeals must be made before the net service is delivered or, if at the end of the game, before the side that appeals has left the court).

APPENDIX 1 — VARIATIONS IN COURT AND EQUIPMENT

1   Where it is not practical to have posts on the sidelines, some method must be used to indicate the position of the sidelines where they pass under the net, e.g., by the use of thin posts or strips of material 1-1/2" side, fixed to the side lines and rising vertically to the net cord.

2.   Where space does not permit the marking out of a court for doubles, a court may be marked out for singles only as shown in Diagram E. The back boundary lines become also the long service lines and the posts or the strips of material representing them shall be placed on the side lines.

APPENDIX 2 — HANDICAP MATCHES

In handicap matches, the following variations in the Laws apply:

1.   No variation is permitted in the number of points required to win a game (i.e., setting the game as in Law 7.4 is not permitted).

2.   Law 8.1.3 will be amended to read: "in the third game, and in a match of one game, when one side has scored half the total number of points required to win the game (the next higher number being taken in case of fractions).

Intermediate and Advanced Skills

7

Following the mastery of sound basic strokes and as experience is gained, additional skills will assure the effectiveness of the fundamentals.

Figure 7-1. Shuttle Scoop

Use the handshake grip with the palm up. Pick up or scoop up a bird lying on the floor, attempting to keep the bird on the racket face. Place your racket face next to the bird with the racket face held nearly parallel to the floor. Slide the racket quickly under the bird with a scooping action allowing the wrist to roll under, catching the bird on the racket face. This is usually done from the right side of the bird for right handers.

DECEPTION

The ability to camouflage shots is a skill very important to a badminton player. All of the basic strokes should look the same up until contact with the shuttle, thus not giving away which shot is coming. The ultimate purpose of developing this deception is to either win the rally outright with a quick, well angled and concealed shot or to force a weak return which can then be put away. Therefore, the basic strokes should be executed with the same preparatory movement. Probably the most important aspect of keeping the same preparatory movement is in the upper body or shoulder turn. Be sure to position the feet the same way and include a vigorous upper body turn on all of the overhead strokes, especially the drop shot. Deception is essential to execute an effective drop shot. Slicing the drop shot will also slow it down, change its direction and add to its deception.

OFFENSIVE OR ATTACKING CLEAR

The attacking clear is a fast or quick clear hit slightly sooner and more out in front of you. It takes a flatter trajectory but high enough so your opponent cannot intercept it before it gets to the back of the court. Often a good drop shot to the net will draw your opponent out of center court and provide the opportunity for the attacking clear to be used successfully.

ADVANCED DROP SHOTS

The fast drop differs from the basic drop shot in that instead of falling from lack of speed straight downward as it reaches the net, it travels deeper into the opponent's court and is quicker, similar to a well angled smash

The crosscourt drop is hit downward with the same preparatory movement as used in the smash. The racket face is tilted slightly in the direction the bird is to travel. You must hit across the bird in a downward direction much like the slice serve in ten-

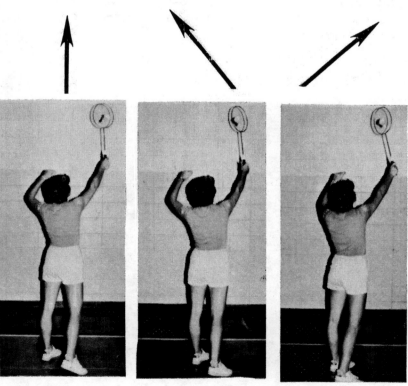

Figure 7-2. Flat or Straight ahead Drop

Figure 7-3. Cross Court Drop-Cut or Sliced

Figure 7-4. Reverse Cut or Sliced Drop

nis. The amount of racket tilt determines how far sideways the bird will go. The crosscourt or slice drop can be hit from both the forehand and the backhand.

Drop shots at the net are softly lifted or "bumped" over as close to the top of the net as possible. The sooner contact is made with these shots the better. The lifting motion should be from the shoulder, not the wrist. The **hairpin dropshot** literally bounces off the face of the racket and falls over the net as shown in Figures 7-5 and 7-6. Another type of dropshot is the **tumble dropshot**. By brushing underneath the bird in a sideways motion, the shuttle will spin or tumble as it goes over the net and will be much more difficult to hit cleanly. The player making the return must allow gravity to straighten the bird's flight back to a perpendicular path in order to contact the tip of the shuttle with their racket.

Figure 7-5. Forehand Drop (Halpin) at Net

Figure 7-6. Backhand Drop at net

The push shot is played at or above the net directing the bird downward to an open spot in your opponent's court. It is pushed, not hit and is highly effective in doubles. The shuttle can be placed past the net player and force the back court player to reach and hit the return up. It also causes some indecision as to who should make the return. The sooner and higher the bird is contacted, the more sharply and steeply all net returns can be made.

ROUND THE HEAD SHOT

This stroke requires the right-handed player to hit the shuttle over the left shoulder. When the bird must be hit over the non-dominant shoulder, the round the head stroke provides a quick, strong return. The body should bend slightly toward the back

**Figure 7-7. Around the Head
Stroke Preparation**

**Figure 7-8. Around the Head
Stroke Execution**

Figure 7-9. Follow-through

hand side with your weight primarily on the nondominant foot but otherwise similar to hitting any normal forehand stroke. The arm swings the racket around behind the head with the forearm almost brushing the head as the arm is extended. The bird should be hit over the left shoulder at the highest possible point. At contact, body weight shifts from the nondominant to the dominant foot on the follow-through. The round the head clear, drop, or smash may be used to return from the backhand side, especially to intercept and quickly return a low clear in that area.

ADVANCED SERVES

If the low doubles serve is higher than it should be or your opponent is rushing quickly, the drive and flick serves can be

Figure 7-10. Drive Serve

Figure 7-11. Flick Serve

used to keep your opponent honest. However both are hit upward and should be used when least expected.

The DRIVEN serve is a low, flat shot usually directed to your opponent's backhand. The speed and unexpectedness of this serve are its chief advantages. It does not give your opponent much time and may result in an outright point. The driven serve should be contacted with the same preparatory motion as the short serve but with vigorous forearm rotation and wrist snap.

The FLICK serve should be sent high enough to clear the receiver's reach but not so high to allow the receiver to get back and make an effective return. The stance and backswing should resemble the short serve but with a quick uncocking of the wrist.

MECHANICAL PRINCIPLES APPLIED TO OVERHEAD STROKES

The angular motion of the levers created by the trunk, shoulder, elbow and wrist is used to give linear motion to the shuttle when it is contacted. The badminton swing in general is not a big one, as in the tennis serve. Power comes from the rapid rotation of the forearm and the extension of the arm from the elbow followed by a vigorous wrist snap. The action of the swing is explosive, particularly in the contact area.

A brief analysis of some of the basic mechanical principles involved in this skill will help to indicate the importance of understanding the applications of these principles. Many other activities involve these and often times other mechanical principles. A list of the most pertinent principles follows, along with some of their applications regarding the badminton overhead strokes:

1. Newton's Law of Inertia
    a. The muscles supply the force to move the body.
2. Newton's Law of Acceleration
    a. Muscular force is necessary to accelerate the arm, wrist and hand.

3. Newton's Law of Action-Reaction
   a. Strings on the racket should be tight.
4. Law of Conservation of Momentum
   a. Shuttle rebounding speed will approximately equal the sum of the racket and shuttle speeds.
5. Velocity = Distance x Time
   a. The overhead smash may reach speeds in excess of 200 mph off of the face of the racket.
6. The angle of refraction equals the angle of reflection.
   a. The racket face must be angled at contact point.
7. Additional force may be gained by bending a joint.
   a. Flexing or cocking the wrist increases linear velocity.
8. A muscle placed on stretch will increase the rate (force) of muscle contraction.
   a. Flexion and extension of the muscles involved in the movement increases their contractile force.
9. The distance that a projectile travels depends upon its initial speed and the angle at which it is projected.
   a. The smash should be hit with force and accuracy.
10. If forces are applied simultaneously, they will be limited by the weakest force of the group of forces.
    a. Strength in the arms, wrists and hands are needed in order to grip the racket adequately.
11. The linear velocity of a projectile can often be increased if angular motion is developed prior to striking.
    a. The speed at which the racket strikes the shuttle is the result of a summation of forces of movement in the trunk, shoulders, arms and wrists.
12. When attempting to apply maximum force to any object by hitting or striking, the body should achieve maximum linear movement in the direction the projectile is to go.
    a. During stroking, body weight is transferred from the back foot to the forward foot.

13. The longer the radius of rotation, the greater the linear velocity.

    a. The racket is an extension of the arm and contact with the shuttle should be made as high as possible.

14. The lighter the object and the larger the surface area, the more it is affected by air resistance.

    a. The badminton "bird" decelerates rapidly. A smash hit initially over 200 miles per hour will lose approximately two-thirds of its speed by the time it reaches the opponent on the opposite side of the net.

15. Eliminating the tendency to decelerate a striking action prior to completion helps one's balance and accuracy and aids in the prevention of injury.

    a. Emphasize correct follow-through in completing the overhead in badminton.

16. In any striking activity, final momentum is of primary importance. Momentum may be transferred from part to whole.

    a. Force is gathered from the push-off of the feet, the rotation of the body, the rotation of the upper extremity and the extension of the arm and hand. These forces are in turn applied to the racket and then the shuttle.

17. When a rigid mass comes in contact with a force, the closer the force is to the center of percussion, the fewer vibrations will be caused.

    a. The shuttle should be contacted in the center of the racket face, known as the sweet spot.

Strategy

8

BASIC SINGLES TACTICS

In singles, you are responsible for your success or failure, for your own good and bad shots. Everyone wants to win, but other important objectives are having fun and exercise. Everyone should win from the standpoint of activity, sportsmanship, and the enjoyment of making some good shots.

Analyze the strengths and weaknesses of your opponent. If he lacks speed or endurance, run him and try to tire him out. Hit the bird away from your opponent, maneuvering him up and back to hopefully force a weak return. Most beginners have not developed a strong backhand, thus hit the majority of shots to that side. If you lack stamina, attack quickly and try to make the rallies short by smashing or trying for outright winners. However, singles is generally a game of patience and running. The clear and drop shot should be most often used. Be aggressive on your service and play safer or more conservative on your opponent's service. Finally, learn the boundaries of the singles court so as not to play returns that would fall out.

BASIC DOUBLES TACTICS

Doubles is very much different from singles. Partners must cooperate, complement each other's strengths and weaknesses,

Figure 8-1. The simplest doubles' method is the side by side.

and enjoy playing together. Do not try to cover too much court or try to make all the shots. Try not to criticize or blame your partner for missed shots or errors. Strategy, strengths, weaknesses, and court coverage should be discussed prior to play.

There are basically three methods to cover the court in doubles: side by side; up and back; and rotational, a combination of the previous two. The simplest method, as shown in Figure 8-1, is the side by side in which the court is split down the center from the net to the baseline, with each partner taking half. The up and back system is usually recommended for mixed doubles with the girl at the net and the man in the back court since he is usually the stronger of the two. The rotational system consists of rotating from up and back to side by side depending on whether you are on offense or defense. The attacking team supposedly has the shuttle directed downward and will fall into a side by side or defending position when either partner is forced to lift the bird upward. Figures 8-2 through 8-5 illustrate the rotational system of court coverage.

Some general suggestions for doubles play are:

1. try to get the bird directed downward

2. help each other by calling "out birds" and "short or long serves"

3. play the bird to the weaker of the two opponents

4. if the bird is returned to your center court, the partner receiving the bird on his forehand should return it.

5. the smash should be utilized as often as possible

ADVANCED SINGLES TACTICS

Advanced badminton singles players should use the clear, the smash, and the drop shot but, in addition, variation and greater skill in their execution is needed. Variation of the serve and its placement is also important. Develop the skill to execute the round the head stroke and the attacking clear if the situation requires it. Quick reflexes and endurance are needed to cover the court, plus accuracy and deception in shot-making.

Since you can score only when serving, the service return in singles is of extreme importance. Since the long serve is essentially a defensive shot, it is important to hit an offensive return that will force your opponent to move but also leave you room for error. The two best methods of return are the attacking clear and the fast drop. A safe, conservative return that keeps your opponent honest is very important.

When receiving a long, high serve in the right court, some good returns are: (1) an attacking clear to your opponent's backhand; (2) a fast drop straight ahead; or (3) a fast crosscourt drop.

When receiving a long, high serve in the left court, some good returns are (1) an attacking clear straight ahead; (2) an attacking clear crosscourt; or (3) a fast drop straight ahead.

The previous suggestions for service return are for a right-handed opponent. If your opponent is left handed, your returns would be the same but from opposite courts.

ADVANCED DOUBLES TACTICS

Doubles play will involve the low serve, the smash, the drive, and net shots. The ultimate purpose of every shot is to cause your opponents to lift the shuttle to you or your partner. In order to score, it is necessary to develop an accurate, low serve from as close to the short service line and center line as possible. This decreases your opponent's angle of return. In doubles, as in singles, a safe, conservative return that will keep opponents honest and cause them to lift their return is important. A choice of one of three returns should be successful. They are: (1) a net drop shot; (2) a push shot; and (3) a midcourt drive. The push shot and the midcourt drive are directed past the "up" partner and force the partner in the back court to reach for and direct the shuttle upward. If the "up" partner does not play aggressive toward the net after serving, then a net drop shot should force him to lift the shuttle. The basic principle is to gain the offensive and keep it.

THE ROTATIONAL OR COMBINATION SIDE-BY-SIDE AND UP-AND-BACK

Figure 8-2. Both teams start in an up and back position when serving or receiving.

Figure 8-3. The team on the left has served short, but the receiver has made a good return forcing the server to clear.

Figure 8-4. The team on the right is now the attacking team (they remain up and back); the team on the left had to hit up and are now on defense.

Figure 8-5. The team on the left is now side-by-side anticipating an offensive return, probably a smash by the attacking team.

Figure 8-6. In normal mixed play, the man served from a deeper position near mid-court. The woman is stationed at the short service line.

Figure 8-7. Following the serve, the man is responsible for any return past the short service line and the woman any in front.

Men's, women's and mixed doubles utilize basically the same strokes, techniques, teamwork and strategy. However, in normal mixed play, both women play close to the net, and the men are responsible for the back court area. Now it is even more important to keep the bird going down. With the women stationed at the net, a drop shot from the back court will in essence be hit right to the woman at the net; any shot hit up will be to her partner in the back court. The half court return or push shot on the return of serve is the safest overall return. And half court and drive shots are the best choice for conventional play patterns in mixed doubles. Figure 8-6 and 8-7 illustrate the positions for mixed doubles play.

Conditioning 9

A badminton player can become a better competitor by being more physically fit. In close matches, fitness usually is a factor in the outcome. The most important considerations in a badminton conditioning program are: 1) muscular strength and muscular endurance; 2) aerobic training or cardiovascular endurance; 3) anaerobic training (interval, circuit and overspeed training); 4) flexibility; 5) concentration; and 6) prevention of injuries. Along with physical exercise to develop the aforementioned factors, a sound diet, adequate sleep, rest and acceptable training rules should be included.

Specific conditioning exercises to develop the areas of fitness previously mentioned are as follows:

1. **Muscular Strength and Muscular Endurance.** Training with weights is an excellent method of developing muscular strength and muscular endurance. A sample weight training program will be outlined at the end of this chapter. The use of relatively heavy weights with a small number of repetitions is recommended for both muscular strength and endurance improvement. Push-ups and/or volleying against a backboard with a covered racket will increase wrist, arm and shoulder strength and endurance. Sit-ups or curl-ups aid in developing abdominal strength and endurance. Rope jumping improves footwork and increases leg strength and endurance.

2. **Aerobic Training or Cardiovascular Endurance.** Running is valuable for muscular and cardiovascular en-

durance. Jogging or distance running, running up and down steps, and rope jumping are all excellent conditioners for aerobic training. Extremely long distance running is probably not necessary for badminton players. A moderately fast pace for 2-4 miles will yield better results than a ten mile run at a very slow pace. Some specific examples are included in the sample circuit training program that follows later.

3. **Anaerobic Training.** Anaerobic training can be accomplished in a number of ways. The ability to change direction quickly is essential in the fast paced game of badminton. Short sprints and shuttle runs requiring a reach, touch, and change of direction are very good for improving one's speed of movement. A recent study determined that during a badminton match, the shuttle is actually in play approximately fifty percent of the time. This indicates that badminton is an intermittent activity with short bursts of activity followed by periods of inactivity, such as, walking around, taking deep breaths, changing courts, et cetera. Even though play is supposed to be continuous, there is a lot of inactivity between points.

   Interval Training duplicates this type of discontinuous activity. It usually involves running intervals with fast runs or sprints followed by periods of relief or rest. Most research indicates that these intervals are best accomplished with a ratio of 1:2, work versus rest. In other words, run a minute and then rest two. Other forms of interval training might involve uphill running, downhill running and/or running steps (bleachers or stairwell). Another example pertains to running laps around an oval track, in which one might run/sprint the straight-a-ways and walk/jog the curves.

   Circuit Training usually involves a series of exercises or stations, each one exercising a specific part of the body spread out over a course or circuit. At each station, one performs a given exercise, then walks, jogs or runs to the next station, where another exercise is performed. The objective is to complete the circuit in a set time (target time) as fast as possible or work for a specific time period at each station (30 seconds, for example). Another consideration is to have several levels of exercises at each station. When one completes the circuit on the first level under the target time, one advances to the next level which may simply be an increased number of repetitions. The target time remains the same. A circuit potentially offers a combination of strength, endurance, flexibility, agility and/or cardiovascular endurance as well. A sample circuit training program is listed as follows:

1. **Beginning** or Level One
   a. 10 jumping jacks
   b. 25 bent knee sit-ups or curl-ups
   c. 100 rope jumps (can be done in two sets of 50)
   d. 10 opposite toe touches
   e. 10 push-ups or 5 minutes on wall volley
   f. five 25 yard sprints or 20 shuttle runs from side line to side line on the badminton court in 2 sets of ten each
   g. walk/run from 1/2 to 1 mile (8:00 to 9:30 minute mile pace)

2. **Intermediate** or Level Two
   a. 15 jumping jacks
   b. 50 bent knee sit-ups or curl-ups
   c. 250 rope jumps (can be done in 5 sets of 50)
   d. 15 opposite toe touches
   e. 15 push-ups or ten minutes on wall volley
   f. five 50 yard sprints or 30 shuttle runs (3 sets of 10 each)
   g. run from 1-2 miles (7:30 to 8:00 minute mile pace)

3. **Advanced** or Level Three
   a. 30 jumping jacks
   b. 150 bent knee sit-ups or curl-ups
   c. 500 rope jumps (5 sets of 100 each)
   d. 30 opposite toe touches

    e. 30 "finger-tip" push-ups or 15 minutes on the wall volley

    f. ten 50 yard sprints or 50 shuttle runs (5 sets of 10)

    g. run from 3-5 miles (6:00 to 7:00 minute mile pace)

Overspeed Training deals with the principle of overload in the area of speed training. This type of training requires someone to go faster than they normally can. An excellent way to accomplish this is with a motorized treadmill by setting the pace faster than you normally can run. For example, you might not be able to run a four-minute mile, but you can probably run a four-minute mile pace for thirty seconds or possibly one minute. Increasing the elevation of the treadmill requires you to exaggerate your knee lift to generate more power. Swinging a tennis racket or swinging a badminton racket under water also provides overspeed training, as well as, utilizing the training principle of specificity. Down-hill and up-hill running are forms of overspeed training. Various forms of **Plyometrics** also emphasize overspeed work. Plyometrics involves bounding, jumping, depth jumping (jumping from a height and rebounding back upwards into the air or to a new height) and rope jumping (using "heavy ropes" or doing double jumps emphasizes power jumping).

4. **Flexibility.** Flexibility refers to the range of movement around a joint. Any stretching activity should help to increase flexibility. Jumping jacks and opposite toe touches are examples of active forms of flexibility exercises. Some research seems to indicate that passive or static stretching is better for you and less likely to cause injury. It usually entails holding the stretch for approximately twenty seconds. Several commercial products are available such as the STRETCH-RITE which is demonstrated in Figures 9-1 through 9-5. This device allows one to hold the stretch longer and without bouncing.

Figure 9-1.
Seated, Single Leg Stretch

Figure 9-2.
Seated, Extended Single Leg Stretch

Figure 9-3.
Standing, Behind Back, Shoulder Stretch

Figure 9-4.
Seated, Both Legs Extended, Sit/Reach

Figure 9-5.
Seated, Straddle Stretch

5. **Concentration.** Concentration is dependent upon one's ability to shut out any outside or extraneous interference. MENTAL PRACTICE might involve reviewing game situations over and over in one's mind or actually perceiving yourself executing good shots and/or winning games. Modern technology allows anyone to watch the very best athletes in any sport. Watching the proper form or tech-

nique of experts on a video tape allows you to observe the correct way to perform the strokes and serves. You may also videotape yourself and see how closely your form resembles theirs. Some studies have gone so far as to edit out all of the improper techniques and only record the strokes that were executed well. Then the subject observes himself or herself performing the stroke correctly. Some research indicates that this type of visual feedback alone, even without physical practice, can improve one's quality of play. Another technique involving mental imagery is to close your eyes and visualize yourself winning or playing well. Finally, RELAXATION seems to also improve one's ability to concentrate and to react more quickly during competition .

6. **Prevention of Injuries.** PROBLEM AREAS or common injuries in badminton include sprains, strains, fractures and cramps. Of all the injuries to which badminton players are prone, those affecting the ankle and/or the foot have the greatest incidence.

A SPRAINED ANKLE is a ligament injury. It results from a sudden twist or rolling over (inversion) of the foot causing the outside (lateral) ligaments to be stretched or torn. Eighty- five percent of all ankle injuries are of this type.

ANKLE FRACTURES are caused by a sudden wrenching or twisting, the same factors that cause sprains; but fractures usually result from excessive force outward (eversion) in relation to the leg.

A STRAIN is a muscle or tendon injury. Landing from jumping exposes the tendons of the ankle and muscles of the foot to the danger of strain. As a badminton player lands, particularly on the overhead motion of the round-the-head shot or the smash, the non-dominant foot absorbs shock three to four times the player's weight. This may give the Achilles tendon a sudden stretch beyond its normal range of motion and thus tear or strain this tendon.

This is a very serious injury that may require surgery, as well as, a long rehabilitation process.

KNEE INJURIES are another common problem faced by badminton players at all levels. When the knee is subjected to the extraordinary stress of running, jumping, lunging, or pivoting (any of which can involve weight loads of up to a thousand pounds), trauma to the knee is a real possibility. The cartilage or meniscus is probably the most often injured component of the knee. This half-moon shaped cushion acts as a shock absorber between the shin (tibia) and the thigh (femur). The old treatment for a torn meniscus was to remove it completely, which entailed hospitalization, a long recovery process and a large scar. However, with the refinement of arthroscopic surgery, a small incision is made through which only the torn part of the meniscus is removed. This allows for a much shorter rehabilitation period of only a few days instead of several months. Another frequent site of knee injury is the ligament. If any of the seven ligaments in each knee is stretched or torn, the knee becomes very unstable. Replacement of the lost ligament tissue with tendon tissue from elsewhere in the body or with Gore-Tex (a synthetic material used to make waterproof rain gear) are potential solutions.

The ELBOW is also particularly susceptible to trauma or stress from repetitive overuse. The overhead throwing motion of both the forehand and the backhand generates a severe whiplash action (particularly, if executed incorrectly) from which soreness can arise due to fatigue and minor strains from overload. TENNIS ELBOW is a popular, generic term covering several different ailments. In general, they are chronic conditions resulting from overuse of certain forearm muscles. They have in common; tenderness about the elbow and pain upon attempting to extend the arm, rotate the forearm, or grip an object.

The SOLUTION to these common injuries suggests that prevention is the best medicine. Sprains and strains to muscles and joints can be reduced by WARMING UP and STRETCHING. A HOT SHOWER can increase one's body temperature, get you loose and possibly prevent a strain. Before playing, one should go through a series of basic stretches. Take a minimum of 5-10 minutes to stretch the ankles and Achilles tendon areas, the hamstring areas, the quadriceps or thigh areas, the back, the shoulders and the arms. All stretches should be done slowly with little or no bouncing. Also include in the warm-up about 5-10 minutes of easy hitting before starting the match. Any injury that produces swelling should be ICED until the swelling is eliminated. The use of HEAT or LINIMENT should be reserved for muscle pulls or strain-type injuries, as well as, for muscle soreness. MASSAGING the tired muscles aids in preventing muscle soreness as well as speeding up one's recovery from fatigue. Research indicates that CRAMPS and muscle soreness can be prevented by keeping the body well hydrated. Drink plenty of LIQUIDS before, during and following heavy exercise. Some of the electrolyte solutions (Gatorade, Powerade and All Sport, for example) seem to prevent muscle soreness if consumed before, during and after exercise. Sugar content, temperature and quantity all affect the speed at which liquids are absorbed by the body. Highly sugared drinks (over 10 percent) are absorbed much more slowly than plain water or low sugar drinks (6-8 percent). Cool water is absorbed faster than tap water or warm drinks. Larger quantities are also absorbed faster. A few swallows of water at the drinking fountain are not absorbed as fast as a large (16-20 ounce) glass of liquid.

Another minor, but extremely uncomfortable injury is the BLISTER. Blisters result from stress on the skin by rubbing or shearing forces that cause friction or heat. Predisposing factors are sweat, shoes that fit poorly, one's style of play and the type of socks used. Use shoes that fit well, socks that absorb moisture and do not wrinkle, as well as, inner soles that cushion shock and PREVENT FRICTION to the feet. Felt, moleskin, foam or foam adhesive pads can be used to cover the more chronic areas of abuse, such as, the balls of the feet. Foot powder also helps. Hands and fingers may also suffer from contact with the racket grip. A soft leather glove or several types of racket grip wraps, tapes or gauzes may cushion the hand from blisters or callouses.

WEIGHT TRAINING

Weight training is specifically designed to develop muscular strength and muscular endurance. In badminton, muscular strength and endurance are needed to move and to execute every stroke.

Generally, the use of heavy loads with a small number of repetitions emphasizes muscular strength development, while relatively light or moderate loads with a larger number of repetitions emphasizes muscular endurance. For the badminton player with little experience in weight training, the following plan is recommended. Select an amount of weight for each exercise that permits 10 to 12 repetitions before fatigue sets in (usually 30 to 50 pounds will suffice for most of the exercises listed). The player then lifts this weight daily or every other day, attempting to increase the number of repetitions. This cycle is repeated indefinitely. As the number of repetitions attained reaches 15 or more, more weight should be added until only 10 to 12 repetitions are possible again. Also, in order to develop and maintain flexibility, each exercise should be performed through a full range of motion around the joints involved. Following are listed several areas that need muscular strength and muscular endurance development.

Hand and Forearm Strength

Pronated Wrist Curls

Grasp a dumbbell at one extreme end and allow it to point downward toward the floor. Then slowly raise the lower end until it points almost directly upward. Keep the arm(s) relatively straight.

Wrist Rolls

Suspend a two and one-half or five pound weight on a 36 inch long nylon rope attached to a cut-off wooden handle approximately one foot long. Roll the hands so that the rope winds around the handle and eventually brings the weight up to and in contact with the handle. Keep the arms extended directly in front of the body at shoulder height. Allow the handle to spin freely returning the weight to its original position and then repeat. See Figures 9-6 and 9-7.

Forehand Wrist Curls

Begin the exercise by picking up the barbell or dumbbells with an underhand or palms up grip. Sit on a bench and extend the hand(s) beyond the knees with the forearms supported on the thighs. Allow the weight to maximally extend the hand(s), then curl the weight to a maximally flexed position. If you do this exercise too fast, the bar or dumbbell may roll past the fingertips and fall to the floor. See Figures 9-8 through 9-9.

Backhand Wrist Curls

Pick up the barbell or dumbbell with an overhand or palms down grip. Seated with the forearms supported on the thighs, flex the hand(s) at the wrist fully and then extend the hand(s) completely backward and upward. Alternate this flexing and extending position.

WRIST ROLLS

Figure 9-6.   Figure 9-7.

FOREHAND WRIST CURLS

Figure 9-8.   Figure 9-9.

Upper Arm and Shoulder Strength

Barbell Curls

Hold the barbell or dumbbells in front of the thighs with the hands spread to shoulder width and palms facing forward, away from the body. Raise the bar to the upper chest by flexing the biceps. Then lower the bar to the starting position and repeat. This exercise can also be performed with the palms down, facing backward for a reverse barbell curl.

Barbell Press

Stand holding the barbell under the chin at chest height with the palms turned upward and facing outward. Press the weight upward over the head until the arms are fully extended. Return to the starting position and repeat.

A slight alteration to the Barbell Press is the Behind the Neck Press. Raise the barbell overhead using the foreward grip. Then slowly lower the bar until it touches the shoulders behind the head and neck. Press to the overhead position and then return the bar slowly to the original starting position in front of the chest and repeat.

Upright Row

Grasp the barbell with the palms down and the hands close together. Lift to the front of the thigh in a standing position. Then pull the barbell to the chin and try to keep the elbows raised as high as possible. Lower the bar slowly and repeat. See Figures 9-10 and 9-11.

UPRIGHT ROW

Figure 9-10.

Figure 9-11.

Triceps Extension

This exercise can be done with one arm only or both arms simultaneously or alternately. Lift the dumbbell overhead to arms length. Then bend the elbow slowly, lowering the weight behind the head until the weight touches the back. Keep the elbow close to the head and straighten the arm, returning the dumbbell to its original position overhead. Two dumbbells are needed if both arms are to be used simultaneously or alternately.

Backhand Side Raises

Start by lying on your non-dominant side on a bench. The dumbbell is held in the dominant hand close to the floor. Using a backhand movement, lift the dumbbell to full extension upward. Then return the weight to the starting position and repeat.

Lateral Arm Raises

Begin by standing with the dumbbell at your side; raise the arm laterally until the weight is overhead. Then lower slowly and repeat.

Horizontal Arm Raises

Standing with the dumbbell at your side, raise the arm forward in front of the body and upward horizontally until the weight is overhead. Then lower slowly and repeat.

Legs

Half Squats

Begin this lift by placing the barbell on the back and shoulders in a standing position. The bar should rest on the shoulders behind the neck. You may wish to wrap the bar in a towel or other soft material to cushion the neck. Sink downward, flexing the knees while keeping the heels flat on the floor. Continue down until the thighs are parallel to the floor. The back should be as flat and straight as possible. Then raise up by straightening the legs to a full, standing position.

Calf Raises

Begin by placing a barbell across the shoulders or by holding dumbbells in your hands. Rise on your toes as high as possible and then drop back down until the heels touch the floor. You can increase the amount of work done by placing the toes and balls of the feet on a slightly raised area, such as might be provided by a short piece of two-by-four lumber. This allows for an even greater distance over which the weight is lifted. See Figures 9-12 and 9-13.

CALF RAISES

Figure 9-12.

Figure 9-13.

SUMMARY

Obviously, there are numerous types of commercial weight training equipment available besides simple dumbbells or free weights. Nautilus, Universal, Keiser, Cybex and Body Masters are only a few of the brand names that can improve muscular strength and muscular endurance through weight training or resistance exercises.

A structured badminton conditioning program varies depending on one's present physical fitness, ability and skill level. Any badminton player can become a better player by being more physically fit. Muscular strength and muscular endurance are important factors in overall fitness. They also aid in improving speed, agility and power on the badminton court.

Practice Drills and Games

10

BASIC DRILLS

Skills suggested for the beginning badminton play include the long serve; the forehand overhead clear, smash and drop shot; the forehand and backhand drives; the short serve; and the net drop shot. Basic drills should emphasize the development of these skills.

Bounce Drill

Following instructions on the grip, the bounce drill is helpful in letting the beginning student get his eye on the bird and get the "feel" of the bird contacting the racket face. The bird is simply bounced off the face of the racket vertically using either the forehand or backhand grip. See Figure 10-1. Another variation is to alternate hitting forehand and backhand bounces in a flip-flop fashion. Continue until each student can bounce the bird 30 times in succession.

Underhand Drill

Following the introduction of the underhand clear, each student should attempt this skill until satisfactorily accomplished. The students should be assembled in a circle, semi-circle, or line formation facing the instructor or center of the circle to practice this stroke.

Figure 10-1. Shuttle Bounce

Overhead Clear Drill

All forehand overhead stroke drills start with two students facing each other from across the net. If possible, have 3-5 shuttles to hit. One player begins the drill by hitting an underhand clear to his partner who in turn hits an overhead clear. From this point on, a rally of overhead clears should continue until 30 clears in succession can be made. Stress controlling the shuttle and directing it high and deep in the court, not in "winning" the rally.

Overhead Smash Drill

Introduce the overhead smash and then have partners alternate hitting underhand clears to each other allowing each partner to hit at least 10 "good" smashes into the partner's court. "Good" smashes are those that land between the short service line and the doubles long service line. Stress "setting the bird up" at mid-court so the partner will have little trouble in experiencing success.

Overhead Drop Shot Drill

This is identical to the overhead smash drill except each partner is to hit at least 10 "good" drops into the partner's court. "Good" drops from back court should travel just over the net and land short of the short service line.

Footwork Drill

This drill requires the student to move quickly about the court similar to movement in an actual game. Stress reaching with the dominant arm and leg; crossing over only on the backhand, not the forehand.

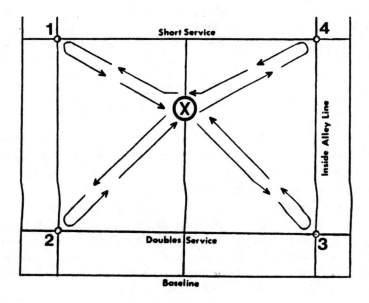

Figure 10-2. Footwork Drill

Starting in the center of the singles' court, touch the four corners of the court in succession and return to the center position after each touch. From center court, move to intersection of: (1) short service line and right side line, then return to midcourt; (2) short service line and left side line, then return to midcourt; (3) baseline and left side line, then return to midcourt; and (4) baseline and right sideline, then return to midcourt. Touch the four corners of the court 20 times following the consecutive numbers with the center being touched after each of the corner touches. It may also be performed for a set time period at maximum speed; for example, the total number of touches that can be obtained in 30 seconds. This is very similar to the Footwork Drill as shown in Figure 10.2.

Short Service Drill

This drill is done with a partner standing in the receiving position returning his partner's low serve with a net drop shot. A continuation of this drill requires both partners to rally at the net with drop shots until an error is made.

Advanced players can use this drill to practice push shot and midcourt drive service returns.

Drive Drill

The drive drill usually begins with the students in circular or semi-circular formation. On both the forehand and backhand drives, the bird is placed on the racket and tossed either to the right or to the left. Stress reaching with the dominant arm and leg; crossing over only on the backhand, not the forehand.

This can be used as a partner drill as well. One partner will set the shuttle up at driving height and slightly deeper than midcourt. One player hits twenty forehand drives, then the procedure is reversed and the other partner has the opportunity to hit. The same procedure is done for the backhand drive.

ADVANCED DRILLS

When practicing the following more advanced drills, it is important for both partners to return to center court after each stroke to simulate as near a game situation as possible.

Advanced Drive Drill

Two partners face each other across the net and hit hard, quick drives directly to one another. A mixture of forehand and backhand are hit with both partners increasing the pace and moving toward the net. As you move closer, the rallies will be quicker and force you to react increasingly faster.

Underhand Clear, Smash and Drop Drill

Partner A sets the shuttle up at smashing height with an underhand clear. Partner B smashes the shuttle at A who in turn defends with a block drop shot. B comes in and clears the shuttle to his partner. This sequence of shots is repeated as long as possible.

Clear and Drop Shot Drill

This drill provides good practice for the two most used singles shots and is an excellent conditioner as well. Partner A hits an underhand clear deep to partner B's forehand. From this position, B drops the shuttle straight ahead to A's backhand. A redrops, B comes in and clears the shuttle out to A's forehand and the sequence continues. Now A will drop straight ahead to B's backhand. B comes in, redrops, and A clears to B's forehand. The rally continues until someone makes an error.

Another version of the previous drill follows exactly the same pattern except upon receiving the deep clear to your forehand, a crosscourt or slice drop is returned instead of the straight drop shot. A starts the rally again by clearing to B's deep forehand. B hits a crosscourt drop to A's forehand who in turn redrops the shuttle. B comes in and clears the shuttle out to A's forehand who follows with the crosscourt drop. B redrops and the rally continues.

Since these drills are for practice, it is important to clear the bird high and deep to give your partner time to set up and hit. Your goal is not to win the rally but to make it last as long as possible.

GAMES

Generally, the large size of most school physical education classes along with limited time and space dictate an emphasis on efficiency.

Half-Court Singles

This game is one that can be played early in the course of the activity. It does not matter who serves, but a point is awarded every time someone makes an error; five 10-point games are recommended.

Net Play Game

Partners are in close to the net and are limited to playing only net drop shots. Again it does not matter who starts the rally, but a point is awarded every time someone makes an error. The shuttle is considered out if it lands past the short service line.

King of the Court

This is a good drill for large numbers and few courts. If three, two or even only one court is available, it is still possible to play Badminton. Acquaint the students to the rules of play. Place one person on each side of the court (teams of 2 or 3 are also acceptable). Remainder of class will await turn at play as either individuals or team. Play begins with one side serving (scoring can be played normally with only serving side scoring or loss of point when either side makes an error or fault). Play one, two or three point "games" in which winner remains on court and next team or individual challenges them. Loser goes to "end of line" to await its next turn of play. If more than one court is available, smaller groups on each court will afford more playing time. This can also provide a ranking or rating scale as determined by total number of points scored and thereby more easily and quickly categorize your class by playing ability.

Speedy-V or Red Bird Special

Various forms of relays or tag team type of play can be instituted. Teams of 9,12, or 15 can be organized and played as individuals or squads of three. When using more than one person on a squad, it is extremely important for them to play an "area" of the court. For example, if three (Speedy-V) are used, have one play up (short service line to the net) and split the back court into halves so that each squad member understands that any shot in his/her area is his/her responsibility. If two team members make up a squad, then simply divide the court in half (either side by side or up and back). Emphasize to them to cover their area only. Every individual or squad plays three points and then rotates (or tags next person or squad to come in). Scoring is by total points for each team. Depending on the number of students in class, game score may be 15 or 21 points. This method provides that no individual or squad can score more than three points at any one time or more especially lose more than three points at any one time. Thus the competition should be more equal.

BEGINNING BADMINTON
IN HIGH SCHOOL

Large high school classes along with limited time and space also dictates an emphasis on the doubles game in badminton instruction. The beginning badminton teacher should select the minimum skills needed to participate in a game and emphasize those skills. Basic skills suggested for a beginning high school badminton unit include the short serve and/or long serve; the forehand overhead clear, smash and drop shot; the forehand and backhand drives; and the hairpin drop at the net.

A suggested course outline for the limited high school situation follows and is structured on a ten-day schedule or lesson plan:

First Day

Introduction—Brief history, safety, care of equipment.

Grip—The forehand grip is sometimes referred to as either the "handshake" or pistol grip. Slide the racket into the hand as if shaking hands with it. The racket should be lying across the palm and fingers with the thumb and index finger forming a V on top of the racket handle. For the backhand, the only change is that the thumb is straight up and down on the top, left-hand bevel of the handle instead of wrapped around it.

Underhand Clear (singles' serve)

Wall Volley Drill—Hit 30 times against flat wall

Bounce Drill—Bounce bird off face of racket vertically 30 times.

Second Day

Review Grip and Clears

Footwork Drill—Starting in center of singles' court, touch the circles located in center and four corners of the court 30 times with racket following the consecutive numbers with the center court being touched after each of the corner touches. STRESS RETURNING TO THE CENTER POSITION.

Play a game of Clears in which it does not matter who serves, but a point is awarded every time someone makes an error; 5-10 point games.

Third Day

Warm-up with 50 clears with partner

Introduce overhead Smash and Drop Shots; alternate hitting underhand clears to your partner allowing him to smash and drop from the back of the court.

Fourth Day

Introduce six item/station circuit drill:

1. Wall Volley—30 times

2. Bounce Hits—30 times

3. Clear—30 overheads with partner

4. Smash—10 "good" smashes that land between short service line and back doubles service line.

5. Drop—10 "good" drops from back court that travel over the net and land short of the short service line.

6. Footwork—30 touches on footwork drill as mentioned on Second Day.

Introduce Forehand and Backhand Drives—Stress reaching with dominant arm and leg; crossover only on the backhand, not the forehand.

Fifth Day

Use Circuit Drill as warm-up; allow two (2) minutes for each station.

Review Forehand and Backhand Drives, again stressing footwork.

Introduce the Low Serve for Doubles.

Introduce the Hairpin Drop Shot at the net, using it as a possible return of the Doubles Serve.

Sixth Day

Circuit Drill

Introduce rules for Doubles play; play 7-10 point games for the remainder of the class.

Seventh Day

Circuit Drill

Review session on Doubles Strategy, including various types or systems of doubles play, such as, up and back, side by side, and rotational (a combination of the previous two).

Play Round Robin Doubles

Eighth Day

Round Robin Doubles (Those not able to play due to lack of court space can be hitting wall volleys and bounce hits.)

Ninth Day

Round Robin Doubles (same as above)

Tenth Day

Evaluation—May consist of a brief written quiz and possibly an objective skill test, such as: total number of wall volleys that can be hit in 30 seconds, total number of touches that can be obtained in 30 seconds on footwork drill, and a short serve test for accuracy.

The designation of badminton as one of the lifetime sports has increased emphasis of badminton skill development in physical education classes and thus provides greater opportunity and enthusiasm for participation in this vigorous activity.

Skill Tests 11

Although skill testing takes time away from actual play, it remains a valuable means of determining one's skill level. By planning carefully and testing students while the rest are practicing or playing games, the amount of time needed can be reduced and used more efficiently.

The following battery of three badminton skill tests developed by Lambert[*] provide valid, reliable and objective measures of badminton playing ability.

LONG SERVE

Subjects should be instructed to stand in the right service court and to serve diagonally to the scoring region, attempting to hit the shuttlecocks above and beyond the rope placed at the ten foot height. The subjects should be allowed three practice serves before hitting the 12 shuttlecocks for which scores will be recorded. Scoring regions and target dimensions are illustrated in Figure 11-1.

The best 10 of 12 trials will be selected for interpretation of data. Serves hit above the waist and shuttlecocks landing outside the scoring region will be scored as zero. Shuttlecocks

---

[*] Lambert, L.C. The construction of a badminton skills text battery for college females and males. Unpublished Master of Science Thesis, Northwestern State University of Louisiana, 1977.

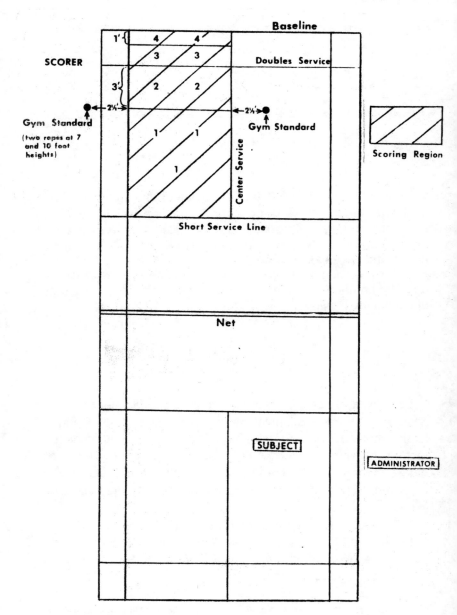

Figure 11-1. Long Serve

passing below the seven foot rope and landing in the service court will receive one point, shuttlecocks passing between the ropes at seven and ten foot heights will be scored according to the scoring region and shuttlecocks going over the rope placed at the ten foot height and landing in the scoring region will obtain the respective numerical values doubled. Any shuttlecocks landing on a scoring or boundary line will be good hits and given the next higher score. Shuttlecocks hitting either rope are to be re-served.

The test administrator should answer questions of the subjects to assure that the test instructions and scoring procedure are clearly understood before testing begins.

WALL VOLLEY

Subjects should practice for 30 seconds before beginning the two test trials and rest for 15 seconds between the two trials. Each subject should be instructed to serve legally from behind the restraining line, and to remain behind the restraining line while volleying. The shuttlecock can be volleyed with any type stroke and only those hits which are struck while standing behind the restraining line and which land in the target area will be counted; the hit will not count if any part of the foot goes over the restraining line. The subject will retrieve and re-serve from behind the restraining line any missed shuttlecocks. Test dimensions and the target area are illustrated in Figure 11-2.

The number of times the subject crosses the restraining line to volley a shuttlecock will be counted by the timer. The counter determines the number of times the shuttlecock hits in the target area. The difference between the two numbers will be the score for the trial. The timer should inform the subject whenever the restraining line is consistently crossed.

The score for the wall volley will be the total number of times the subject hits the shuttlecock in the target area, while standing behind the restraining line, for the two 30 second trials.

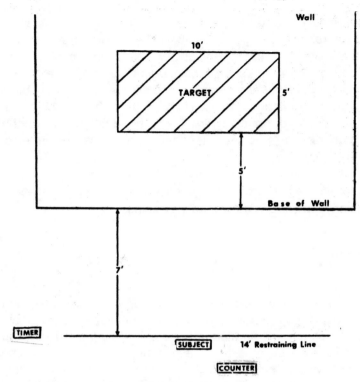

Figure 11-2. Wall Volley

Questions from the subjects concerning test directions or scoring procedure must be answered before testing begins.

FOOTWORK-AGILITY DRILL

The subjects should be directed to begin at the starting position with the head of the badminton racket on the center touch spot located two feet in front of the starting position, as

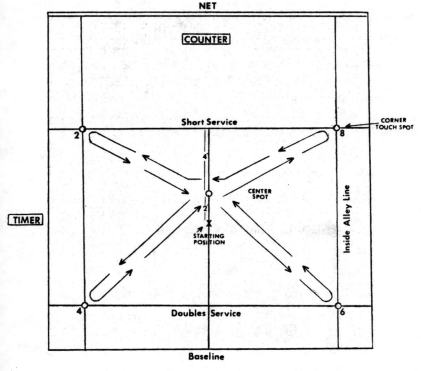

Figure 11-3. Footwork — Agility Drill

illustrated in Figure 11-3. The timer should give the signal "ready go" at which time the subject, with racket in the dominant hand, should make as many touches as possible in a 30 second period at the corner and center touch spots. The subject should move to the left front corner proceeding in a counterclockwise direction, returning to the starting position and touching the center spot each time as indicated by the arrows and numbers in Figure 11-3. The test administrator should walk through the circuit twice as a demonstration.

The score for the skill test will be the number of touches made in a 30 second period with the total count including the touching of the center touch spot. Subjects should be informed that the spots must be touched to receive a score and that no score will be given for hitting close to the spot. Each subject has the option of returning to and touching a missed spot or continuing through the circuit.

Each subject should walk through the circuit twice to assure that the test directions are understood correctly.

Glossary

Alley. Playing area on each side of the court 1 1/2 feet wide between the doubles side line and the singles side line.

Badminton World Federation. The current world governing body for badminton.

Back Alley. An area 2 1/2 feet deep between the doubles back service line and the baseline.

Backhand. Stroke hit on the left side of the body by right-handed players.

Backswing. That part of the swing which takes the racket back in preparation for the forward swing.

Base. A spot on the middle line, slightly closer to the net than the baseline, to which, in singles, you should try to return after most shots.

Baseline. A line designating the back boundary of the court.

Bird. The missile used in badminton; same as shuttle or shuttlecock.

Clear. A high shot which goes deep into the back court.

Crosscourt. A stroke which sends the bird diagonally across the court.

Double Hit. The shuttle is hit twice in succession on the same stroke. A fault.

Drive. A stroke that sends the bird in a relatively flat trajectory at a high rate of speed.

Drive Serve. A hard, fast serve which crosses the net with a flat trajectory. The shuttle is usually directed toward the receiver's left shoulder. A shot used in doubles play for the most part.

Drop Shot. A stroke hit underhand or overhand from a point in the court away from the net which barely clears the tape and falls nearly vertically.

Fault. Any violation of the rules.

Flick. An especially quick movement of the wrist, accompanied by little arm motion, that sends the bird high and toward the rear of the opponent's court.

Flick Serve. A serve with which the shuttlecock is sent into the back court with a quick uncocking of the wrist. Used in doubles if the receiver is consistently rushing your short serve.

Follow-Through. The smooth continuation of a stroke after the racket has met the bird.

Forecourt. The front part of the court.

Forehand. Stroke hit on the right side of the body by right-handed players.

Front Service Line. Line parallel to, and $6^1/2$ feet from, the net on each side of the court, forming the forward boundary of the service courts.

Game. A ladies' singles game consists of 11 points; men's singles, ladies' doubles, men's doubles and mixed doubles consist of 15 points.

High Serve. A serve hit high and deep into the receiver's half court.

I.B.F. International Badminton Federation. The former world governing body of badminton. See Badminton World Federation.

Inning. A side's serving turn.

Let. Point is replayed.

Love. In scoring, nothing or zero.

Match. Best two out of three games.

Match Point. The point which wins the match.

Mixed Doubles. A four-handed game in which a man and a woman play as partners on each side.

Net Shot. A form of drop shot or sharply struck shot played from a point near the net.

Overhead. A stroke played from a point above head height.

Overhead Clear. A shot in which the shuttle is contacted above head height and travels high and deep into the back court.

Overhead Drop Shot. A softly h it overhead stroke which falls just over the net in the opponent's court.

Placement. A shot hit to the specific place in the opponent's court where it will be difficult to return.

Position. The point at which a player stands on the court at a particular time during a rally.

Push Shot. A shot hit gently down into the opponent's court.

Rally. The exchange across the net between sides before the end of a particular point.

Receiver. Player who receives the serve.

Return. The hitting back of an opponent's shot.

Round the Head. An overhead smash stroke, using the forehand grip, played from the vicinity of the left shoulder.

Serve. The act of putting the bird in play at the beginning of a rally.

Server. Player who delivers the serve.

Service Court. One of the two half courts into which the service must be directed.

Service Over. Loss of serve, service goes to opponent or opponents.

Setting. Method of increasing the game points when the score is tied at 9 all or 10 all in women's singles play; 13 or 14 all in doubles play and men's singles play.

Short or Shallow. A shot which does not go as deep into the court as the hitter intends—such as a clear which only goes to midcourt or a serve that does not reach the short service line.

Shuttle, Shuttlecock. See Bird.

Smash. A stroke hit downward with great speed and power.

Stroke. Act of hitting the bird with the racket.

Thomas Cup. Men's international competition is similar to the Davis Cup in tennis and was first held in 1948. Six singles and three doubles matches are played. Thomas Cup competition is held every three years.

Uber Cup. The Uber Cup Women's international competition was started in 1957. This cup is named for a former English player, Mrs. H.S. Uber. Uber Cup competition is held every three years.

USA Badminton. The former United States Badminton Association. USA Badminton is now is the governing body for badminton in the U.S.

Wood Shot. The shot which results when the base of the shuttle is hit by the frame of the racket rather than by the strings. Although they have not always been legal, the IBF ruled in 1963 that wood shots were acceptable.

Evaluation and Records

The evaluation forms and records which follow are designed for estimating progress and indicating areas which need work. In addition, a record of outside class participation is recommended.

BADMINTON SKILL RATING

Forehand

1. Correct grip and ready position   1   2   3   4   5
2. Movement into hitting stance
   (footowrk, side turned to net, etc.)   1   2   3   4   5
3. Weight transferred into shot   1   2   3   4   5
4. Forearm rotation (wrist allowed to uncock naturally   1   2   3   4   5
   with arm fully extended at contact)
5. Follow-through   1   2   3   4   5
6. Contact point, angle and placement:
   - a. Clear   1   2   3   4   5
   - b. Smash   1   2   3   4   5
   - c. Drop Shot   1   2   3   4   5
   - d. Drive   1   2   3   4   5

Backhand

1. Correct grip and ready position   1   2   3   4   5
2. Movement into hitting stance   1   2   3   4   5
3. Weight transferred into shot   1   2   3   4   5
4. Forearm rotation   1   2   3   4   5
5. Follow-through   1   2   3   4   5
6. Contact point, angle and placement:
   - a. Clear   1   2   3   4   5
   - b. Smash   1   2   3   4   5
   - c. Drop Shot   1   2   3   4   5
   - d. Drive   1   2   3   4   5

Serve

1. Correct starting stance   1   2   3   4   5
2. Position on court
   - a. Singles   1   2   3   4   5
   - b. Dougles   1   2   3   4   5
3. Weight transferred omtp serve   1   2   3   4   5
4. Forearm rotation/wrist action
   - a. Singles   1   2   3   4   5
   - b. Dougles   1   2   3   4   5
5. Contact below waist/angle/placement
   - a. Singles   1   2   3   4   5
   - b. Doubles   1   2   3   4   5
6. Follow-through   1   2   3   4   5

RECORD OF PLAY

Time & Date	Opponent	Score	Strengths	Weak-nesses	Other Comments

OUTSIDE CLASS PARTICIPATION

Intramurals _____

_____

_____

_____

_____

_____

Tournament Play (local, regional, etc.) _____

_____

_____

_____

_____

_____

Observation _____

_____

_____

_____

_____

_____

Miscellaneous _____

_____

_____

_____

_____

Selected References

Appendix 3

BOOKS

Ballon, Ralph. (1992) *Badminton for Beginners,* Morton Publishing Company, Englewood, Colorado.

Bloss, Margaret V., (1991) *Badminton.* Brown Publishing Co., Dubuque, Iowa.

Paup, Don and Jim Breem (1993) *Winning Badminton.* The Ronald Press Co., 79 Madison Ave., New York, N.Y.

Hashman, Judy. *Badminton, A Champion's Way.* 20 Sandleigh Road, Wootton, Berkshire, England.

Poole, James, *Badminton.* Goodyear Publishing Co., Inc., Pacific Palisades, California, 09272.

Rogers, Wynn. *Advanced Badminton.* Brown Co., Publishers, Dubuque, Iowa.

Reznick, Jadk and RonByrd. (1987). *Badminton,* Gorsuch Scarisbrick Publishers, Scottsdale, Arizona.

Sports Illustrated Book of Badminton, The Editors of Sports Illustrated, J.B. Lippincott Co., E. Washington Square, Philadelphia, Pa., 19105.

MAGAZINES AND GUIDES

Badminton Gazette, official publication of Badminton Association of England, 24 The Charter Road, Woodford Green, Essex, England.

Badminton Review, Canadian Badminton Association, 2 Rochmond St., Charlottetown, P.E.I., Canada.

Badminton USA, official publication of the United States Badminton Association, 1750 East Boulder Street, Colorado Springs, Colorado 80909.

Ideas for Badminton Instruction, Lifetime Sports Education Project, 1201 Sixteenth St., N.W., Washington, D.C., 20036.

Tennis-Badminton Guide, Division for Girls' and Women's Sports, American Alliance for Health, Physical Education and Recreation, 1201 Sixteenth St., N.W., Washington, D.C. 20036.

World Badminton, official publication of International Badminton Federation, Secretary, I.B.F., 24 Winchcombe House, Winchcombe Street, Sheltenham, Gloucestershire, GL52 2NA, England

VIDEOS AND FILMS

Assorted Badminton Video, USBA Office, 1750 East Boulder Street, Colorado Springs, CO 80909.

Beginning Badminton Series, Athletic Institute, 805 Merchandise Mart, Chicago, Ill., 60654.

Badminton Fundamentals, Coronet Instructional Films, 65 E. S. Water St., Chicago, Ill., 60601.

"Badminton: One of the World's Fastest Sports," Vic Braden Promotional Badminton Video.

1991-1994 U.S. Open Championships (USBA)

1991-1994 National Championships (USBA)

Evaluation Questions

True-False: Circle "T" if the statement is true; circle "F" for false statements.

SECTION A — FUNDAMENTALS

T   F   1.   The generally accepted earliest origin of the badminton game is India.

T   F   2.   The net is 5'1" high at the center.

T   F   3.   One should reach as high as possible for overhead shots.

T   F   4.   Gut strings are less expensive and more durable.

T   F   5.   Most of the power in the backhand stroke comes from rotating the forearm.

T   F   6.   The forehand grip in badminton is similar to the Eastern forehand grip of tennis.

T   F   7.   A violation of the rules in badminton is termed a fault.

T   F   8.   It is possible to hit all the same shots with the backhand and the forehand.

T   F   9.   When gripping the racket, the fingers should be bunched as in gripping a hammer.

T   F   10.   The United States Badminton Federation is the governing body for badminton in the U.S.

T   F   11.   Most badminton shots should be hit with the arm fully extended at contact.

T   F   12.   The "round the head" shot can be used in place of the backhand.

T   F   13.   The thumb curves around the handle of the racket on the backhand grip.

T   F   14.   The flight of the shuttle is low and flat over the net for the singles serve.

T   F   15.   In overhead strokes, the weight is on the forward foot during the backswing.

T   F   16.   In almost all strokes, the follow-through of the racket is in line with the shuttle path.

T   F   17.   The shuttle should drop virtually straight down in the back of the court for the long serve.

T   F   18.   The slowest of the nylon shuttles is designated by a red band.

T   F   19.   Directing the shuttle to a specific spot on the court is called placement.

T   F   20.   The drive is a powerful stroke hit downward.

T   F   21.   Good footwork requires bouncy or sliding steps to get into position.

T   F   22.   The most important single stroke is the serve.

T   F   23.   The forehand grip is sometimes referred to as the pistol grip.

T   F   24.   The racket face is parallel to the floor when the player grasps the racket with the forehand grip.

T   F   25.   All badminton rackets need to be stored in a press when not in use.

SECTION B — RULES AND SCORING

T   F   1.   It is illegal for a player to return the shuttle while standing outside the court.

T   F   2.   It is legal for a player's racket to follow through over the net.

T   F   3.   A player is deemed ready if he attempts to return a serve.

T   F   4.   During the serve, when the receiver's foot is on the line, it is considered in the court.

T   F   5.   A team can decline setting a game at 29-all.

T   F   6.   If the partner of the receiver hits the served shuttle, a point is scored for the serving side.

T   F   7.   In doubles, no person should receive two consecutive serves.

T   F   8.   Badminton is like racquetball in that only the serving side may score.

T   F   9.   Setting was designed to eliminate the server's advantage in a game.

T   F   10.   A shuttle that lands on the line is out of the court.

T   F   11.   On the serve, a shuttle may legally strike the net.

T   F   12.   A serve in singles that lands in the side alley is good.

T   F   13.   The head of the racket must be level with or below the hand during service.

T   F   14.   When the score reaches 20-all in a 21 point game, the receiving team has the option to set the game.

T   F   15.   A service is considered to be delivered when the receiver contacts the bird.

T   F   16.   It is never legal for your racket to be on the other side of the net.

T   F   17.   Although the server must have both feet in contact with the floor, the receiver may be moving.

T   F   18.   The server may have a feinting or faking motion during the serve to try to deceive the receiver.

T   F   19.   Striking the shuttle with the frame of the racket is a fault.

T   F   20.   It is legal to contact the bird on your opponent's side of the net.

T   F   21.   In singles, the service starts in the right hand court at the beginning of the game.

T   F   22.   In singles, if your score is an even number, your service is from the left court.

T   F   23.   A point is scored whenever a fault is committed.

T   F   24.   Partners must alternate returning the bird in doubles.

T   F   25.   The winner of the first game serves first at the beginning of the second game.

SECTION C — FOOTWORK AND STRATEGY

T   F   1.   Footwork is essential in getting the body in position to make an effective stroke.

T   F   2.   When playing singles, after each stroke, the player should attempt to return to the middle of the court.

T   F   3.   To return a shot, a player should wait until the shuttle crosses the net and then move into position as quickly as possible.

T   F   4.   On almost all strokes, one should reach with the dominant leg at the same time they reach with the racket.

T   F   5.   A good stroke to use to give a player time to get back into position is the drop shot.

T   F   6.   Whenever possible, returns should be directed to an opponent's weakness.

T   F   7.   It is good strategy to vary placement and types of shots.

T   F   8.   The long serve should be used more frequently in singles play.

T   F   9.   The playing formation usually used in mixed doubles is the side by side.

T   F   10.   A player gains the offensive when forcing the opponent to return upwards.

T   F   11.   A smash is effective when executed from the back of the court.

T   F   12.   When playing the rotation system of doubles, the team is put on the defensive. They should now take a side by side position.

T   F   13.   In doubles, one wants to get the bird directed upward to the opponent.

T   F   14.   The smash should be used more often in singles than in doubles.

T   F   15.   A singles strategy for badminton is to hit the bird away from your opponent.

T   F   16.   The clear and the drop shot should probably be most often used in singles play.

T   F   17.   The clear should be used as little as possible during a rally in doubles.

T   F   18.   It is best to move your opponent, trying to force a weak return that can be smashed.

T   F   19.   The up and back formation in doubles is a poor defensive system.

T   F   20.   All of the basic strokes should look the same up until contact with the bird is made.

T   F   21.   In doubles, help your partner by calling shots that will land out of bounds.

T   F   22.   If a bird is returned to center court, the partner receiving the bird on his forehand should return it.

T   F   23.   The simplest method of covering the court in doubles is the side by side system.

T   F   24.   In doubles, play the bird to the weaker of the two opponents.

T   F   25.   Most beginners have developed a strong backhand, therefore, the majority of your returns should be hit away from that side.

SECTION D — INTERMEDIATE/ADVANCED

PART ONE: **Short Answer**. In the spaces provided, answer the following questions and complete the following statements in as few words as possible.

1. In a _____ shot, the shuttle should pass close to the top of the net.

2. When playing singles, after each stroke the player should attempt to return to _____ .

3. A smash is not effective when executed from _____ .

4. In announcing the score, whose score is given first? _____ .

5. How does play continue when a player, while serving, swings at the shuttle and completely misses it? _____

6. When is a serve considered to be delivered? _____

7. In doubles, which team serves first at the beginning of the second game? _____

8. In a singles game the server has an even score. From which court will she serve? _____

9. When do partners on the "in" side change service courts? _____

10. What is the score in women's singles when a 60-second interval may be taken? _____

11. What is the decision in the following situation? Both players on one side of the net touch the shuttle and it goes over the net within the playing boundaries of the opponent's court. _____

12. What is the decision in the following situation? "A" serves a shuttle which would have gone out of bounds. Her opponent, "B", returns it. _____

13. What happens if a player swings at a shuttle but misses it and the shuttle lands out of bounds? _____

14. A shuttle falling on a line is _____ .

15. The best two out of three games is called _____ .

16. If a third game is played, players change sides of the net when one side has a score of _____ .

17. When a game is played without an umpire, the score is announced by _____ .

18. The score when neither person or team has any points" is
   _____ .

19. If, during a rally, the shuttle after passing over the net is
   caught in the net it is _____.

20. An indistinct hit or sliding contact between the racket and
   shuttle is called _____.

21. Directing the shuttle to a specific spot on the court is
   called _____.

22. Any stroke used in returning a shuttle from the non-racket
   side of the body is called _____.

23. The name for an alert position assumed by a player when
   waiting for the shuttle to be hit by an opponent is
   _____ .

24. A four-handed game is called _____.

25. During the rally, a shot from the player's right court to the
   opponent's right court is called _____.

26. An intermediate attacking stroke between an overhead and
   underhand shot is _____.

27. A player gains the offensive when she has forced her
   opponent to direct the flight of the shuttle. _____

28. When a shuttle is hit from a height and falls almost per-
   pendicularly, just over the net, the stroke is called _____ .

29. A good stroke used to give a player time to get back into
   position is _____.

30. A long service, in singles, to be effective should be
   _____.

31. and _____.

32. In doubles, the person playing net should stand near the
   _____.

33. In doubles, when the serve changes from one partner to another, it is called _____ .

34. The type of doubles play in which each player is responsible for covering one half of the court from the net to the back service line is called _____.

35. The playing formation usually used in mixed doubles is the _____ .

36. In singles, after having been forced deep in the court to return a shuttle, the player should attempt to move to _____ .

37. The serve used most frequently in singles is the _____.

38. In covering court, three acceptable ways of using the feet are _____,

39. _____ .

40. and _____ .

PART TWO: Multiple-Choice Decisions: Each of the following statements presents a situation which requires one of the following five decisions. Place the code letter that corresponds to the correct decision in the space provided.

>   CODE: (A) Point for "A"
>   (B) for "B"
>   (C) Continue Play
>   (D) Replay the Point

_____ 41. "A" serves from the left service court and "B", the receiver, contacts the shuttle but claims she was not ready.

_____ 42. "A" begins her serve and at the same instance a spectator throws a cup onto the court. "A's" serve falls into the net.

_____ 43. "A" is serving in singles. The shuttle goes over "B's" head and lands on the base line.

_____ 44. "A" serves and the shuttle touches the net and goes over into the correct service court. "B" lets the shuttle touch the floor.

_____ 45. In a rally in doubles "B" swings at the shuttle and misses; her partner hits the shuttle over the net and within the boundaries.

_____ 46. Team "A" serves, later returns the shuttle to "B's" court. "B" barely touches the shuttle and "B's" partner hits the shuttle over the net.

_____ 47. The score is 3-2 in a doubles game with "B" serving. The server misses the shuttle in attempting to serve.

_____ 48. "A" serves in singles. Later during a rally "B" swings at the shuttle and misses it. The shuttle lands outside the singles side lines.

_____ 49. "A" and "B" are playing singles. "A" serves. In a rally at the net "A's" racket touches the net but the bird goes over the net and "B" misses it.

_____ 50. "A" and "B" are playing singles. "A" serves and "B" returns the shuttle which goes outside of "A's" singles side lines. "A" goes off of the court and returns the bird.